GCSE Edexcel Religious Studies
Religion and Society
(Unit 8)
The Revision Guide

Want to hear the **bad news**? There's an awful lot of heavy-going
stuff they expect you to learn for GCSE Religious Studies.

Want to hear the **good news**? Good old CGP have got it all covered!
We've produced this brilliant book, with all the key concepts explained
in clear, simple English so you can understand it — and remember it.

And then, in the spirit of going the extra mile, we've put in
a smattering of not-so-serious bits to try and make the
whole experience at least partly entertaining for you.

We've done all we can — the rest is up to you.

What CGP is all about

Our sole aim here at CGP is to produce the highest quality
books — carefully written, immaculately presented and
dangerously close to being funny.

Then we work our socks off to get them out to you
— at the cheapest possible prices.

Contents

Section Four — Crime and Punishment

Bible / Qur'an References

References from the Bible always go in the order: *Book Chapter:Verse(s)*. So whenever you see something like: *Mark 3:5-6*, it means it's from the book of Mark, Chapter 3, Verses 5-6.

Similarly, references from the Qur'an are shown with the *Surah (Chapter)* followed by the *Ayat (Verse)*.

Published by Coordination Group Publications Ltd

Editors:
Sharon Keeley, Luke von Kotze, Andy Park, Julie Wakeling

Contributors:
Maria Amayuelas-Tann, Paul D. Smith

ISBN: 978 1 84762 303 4

With thanks to Mary Falkner and Karen Gascoigne for the proofreading.
With thanks to Laura Phillips for the copyright research.

Groovy website: www.cgpbooks.co.uk

Jolly bits of clipart from CorelDRAW®

Printed by Elanders Hindson Ltd, Newcastle upon Tyne

Your Opinions Matter

Welcome to Religious Studies — it may be <u>a little bit different</u> from the subjects you've studied before. This book covers half of the full course GCSE, or the whole of the short course GCSE. You get lots of <u>options</u> for RS, so make sure you've got the right book before you start.

In RS you get <u>Marks</u> for <u>More</u> than just <u>Knowledge</u>

In GCSE Religious Studies there are two 'assessment objectives' — these are the skills you'll need to show to get marks in the exams. You get <u>half</u> your marks for each.

1) The first gives you marks for <u>describing</u> and <u>explaining</u> what you <u>know</u>.
2) The second gives you marks for making <u>arguments</u> backed up with well-thought-out <u>reasoning</u> — and for <u>understanding</u> and <u>explaining</u> other people's opinions.

What <u>You Think Matters</u>...

1) So unlike most of the other subjects you might have exams on (such as maths), in RS you're supposed to <u>think</u> about what you're learning and come to your own <u>conclusions</u>.
2) A lot of the topics you study are pretty controversial — such as capital punishment. In RS you have to decide where <u>you</u> stand on these <u>difficult issues</u>.
3) In fact, being able to give reasoned <u>opinions</u> will count for <u>half</u> your <u>marks</u>.

In my opinion — that is an awesome hat.

...But You've Still Got a <u>Lot</u> to <u>Learn</u>

1) Unfortunately, you can't just weigh in with opinions based on how you feel that afternoon. In the exam you have to <u>back up</u> what you say with <u>reasons</u>. Those reasons will be what you've <u>learnt</u> during the course.
2) You'll also need to know the <u>reasons</u> why some people might <u>disagree</u> with you. In other words, you'll have to present <u>both sides</u> of an argument.
3) And don't forget, the other half of your marks comes from just <u>knowing things</u>. As much as you need to be able to argue, you'll still need to learn all the basics — what things <u>mean</u> and what different people <u>believe</u>.

There'll be <u>Fact Questions</u> and <u>Opinion Questions</u>

So in the exam you'll get questions like:

> What is Situation Ethics?

For these you have to give the definitions of the words you've learnt. There's a <u>glossary</u> in the back that should help you learn them.

As well as questions like:

> Do you agree with organ transplants? Give two reasons for your point of view.

For which you'll need to give your own <u>opinion</u> — backed up with reasons.

And some like:

> Choose one religion and explain its teachings on war.

For these you'll need to give <u>details</u> about the religion(s) you've studied.

And some questions will ask you to: Give reasons why some people may disagree with you.

This means for each topic you're going to have to:
1) <u>Learn</u> the <u>facts</u>.
2) Work out what <u>you think</u> and <u>why</u>.
3) Learn <u>why</u> people might <u>disagree</u> with you.

What do you think of it so far?

It turns out that you have to do twice as much as you might have thought. First you've got to commit each topic to memory, and then you have to figure out what your take on it is. I guess in some ways it's unavoidable, given that this course is about what people <u>believe</u>. And I believe it's about time for some Religious Studies — oh yes.

Christian Morals and Ethics

Quick — do French instead. No... okay, you have been warned...

Morals — What's Right and What's Wrong

1) A person's idea of moral truth is what they believe to be right and wrong.

2) Different people will have different views on the morals of a particular situation. For example, one person might think, *"It's always wrong to lie,"* whereas another person might think, *"It's generally wrong to lie, but if a lie will stop someone getting hurt unnecessarily, then it's okay."*

3) Christians are likely to look for moral guidance from:

   - The Bible — both the Old and the New Testaments.
   - The Church (the Christian community) — either by taking advice from a local minister or by following the teachings of an institution (e.g. the Roman Catholic Church).
   - Their own conscience.
   - Situation Ethics — the principle that there are no straightforward 'rights' and 'wrongs', apart from the commandment to "love your neighbour as yourself".

The Bible is a Christian Moral Guidebook

Christians accept the Bible as authoritative in forming their beliefs and guiding their actions.

1) Christians believe the Bible offers directions for living a moral life, and that it presents Jesus Christ as our example for godly living.

2) But different groups of Christians interpret the Bible in different ways:

   Fundamentalism Fundamentalists believe that the Bible is the direct word of God, so it's wrong to question anything it says. Many fundamentalists base their moral judgements wholly on the teachings of the Bible.

   Conservative View This view is probably the most common among Christians. They believe that the Bible was inspired by God but not dictated — that it was influenced by the writers' own interests and the social background of the time. Readers must use their intelligence, their conscience and the guidance of the Holy Spirit to help them interpret the Bible's moral teachings. Many Roman Catholics trust to the Pope and the Magisterium (see next page) to interpret the Bible for them.

The Ten Commandments — show some Respect

Jesus was a Jew, so his values were grounded in Jewish belief. The most famous moral laws in the Jewish Old Testament are the Decalogue (i.e. the Ten Commandments):

From Exodus 20:
You shall have no other gods before me.
You shall not bow down before idols.
You shall not misuse the name of the Lord.
Observe the Sabbath and keep it holy.
Honour your father and mother.

You shall not murder.
You shall not commit adultery.
You shall not steal.
You shall not give false testimony (lie).
You shall not covet (want someone else's stuff).

Basically the Ten Commandments are about showing respect — to God, and to other people.

You shall learn all this stuff properly...

For some Christians, the word of the Bible is absolute. If the Bible says something's wrong, then it's wrong — and to question that teaching is disrespectful to God. But others argue that there are contradictions in the Bible, so it's impossible to take everything at face value. Tricky. And that's where the Church comes in...

Christian Morals and Ethics

Churches have a Powerful Influence on their Followers

The Pope has a massive influence over Roman Catholics.

Mimmo Chianura/Rex Features

1) Some Christians look to religious <u>leaders</u> (e.g. the Pope or the Archbishop of Canterbury) and religious <u>traditions</u> to find moral truth.

2) Church leaders are <u>respected</u> and <u>trusted</u> by faithful followers.

3) So the teachings of Churches (particularly the Roman Catholic Church) exert a strong <u>influence</u> on issues like infertility and genetic engineering.

4) Many Churches also influence <u>social</u> and <u>political</u> development through involvement in peace and justice movements.

The Magisterium — this is the <u>teaching authority</u> of the Pope and bishops of the Roman Catholic Church.

1) To Roman Catholics, the authority of the <u>Church</u> rivals that of the Bible itself.

2) The Pope is believed to be <u>infallible</u> on questions of faith and morals (i.e. he <u>can't</u> make a mistake).

3) <u>Dogmas</u> are firm beliefs of the Catholic church — some come from the Bible, but some are Church <u>traditions</u> (e.g. the belief that the Virgin Mary was born without sin). Most of them are set out in a series of statements called the <u>Catechism</u>, to help its members understand what they should believe.

But religious leaders are <u>human</u>, and humans have <u>failings</u> — so can Christians trust that they speak for God? The same goes for the <u>traditions</u> of the Church. All religious institutions were founded by <u>humans</u>.

Some Christians Always Follow their Conscience

1) Your <u>conscience</u> is that little voice in your head telling you what's right or wrong.

2) Some Christians argue that this is the <u>voice of God</u>, so we should listen to it very carefully and <u>always trust</u> what it's telling us.

3) Others say that it's just the result of your <u>upbringing</u> — e.g. your parents' opinions, things you've read or heard, religious teachings...

4) If this is true, then your conscience is <u>only</u> as trustworthy as the things it's based on.

A little voice told Kevin it was wrong...

Situation Ethics is all about Showing the Greatest Love

1) Situation Ethics is a Christian principle based on the idea that the only <u>intrinsically good</u> thing is <u>Christian love</u> — that is an unselfish, absolute and unconditional love for all people.

2) The principle states that <u>all decisions</u> should be made to achieve the <u>greatest amount</u> of love. So any Biblical or Church law can be broken, if breaking it results in <u>more love</u>.

3) This is quite a <u>hard</u> thing to get your head around, because the sort of love we're talking about isn't <u>cuddly</u> or <u>sentimental</u>. These decisions are usually about causing the <u>least harm overall</u>.

4) Here are a few <u>real examples</u> of where Situation Ethics could come into play:

  • A homeless man steals a loaf of bread to feed himself.
  • A widow marries someone she doesn't love, but who will care for her children.
  • A dictator is murdered to end a harsh regime.
  • Tens of thousands of civilians die, to end a war that had killed millions *(Hiroshima)*.

5) In each case, from the perspective of '<u>greatest love</u>', it could be argued that the <u>end</u> justifies the <u>means</u>.

The most loving thing isn't always the nicest...

In practice, most Christians base their moral judgements on a combination of lots of different sources. But respect and love are the <u>basic principles</u> of Christianity, and they're a good place to start when you're looking for answers to complex moral questions. Not that they give any <u>easy</u> answers, mind you...

4

Human Rights

Human rights are the moral, legal and political rights that ought to apply to every human being on Earth. They give basic freedoms, e.g. freedom from violence, and protection, to people around the world.

The United Nations Defined Human Rights in 1948

1) In 1948, the United Nations (UN) published the Universal Declaration of Human Rights. The aim was to lay down minimum rights for every person, in every country in the world.

2) It states that all human beings are born free and equal in dignity and rights. It also contains 'articles' that lay down specific rights, e.g. the right to life, freedom from slavery, freedom from imprisonment or exile without good reason, freedom of opinion and expression, the right to seek work and to receive an education.

3) The Universal Declaration of Human Rights is a statement of the way things ought to be, but means nothing in a court of law. So in 1953, the Council of Europe brought into effect its European Convention on Human Rights. This is a similar list of rights that's enforceable by the European Court of Human Rights in Strasbourg.

The European Court of Human Rights in Strasbourg. (I think.)

4) These rights became part of the UK's domestic law in 1998, with the Human Rights Act.

   1) This act protects the human rights of UK Citizens under UK law.
   2) Most of the rights in the Human Rights Act are limited. That means a person's rights can be restricted to prevent a crime or protect the rights of others.
   3) The rights of the wider community are put before the rights of one individual.

Most Christians Strongly Support Human Rights

Basic human rights are a really important idea for many Christians. Whatever their denomination (Roman Catholic, Anglican, Methodist, etc.) most Christians agree that:

1) All human beings are equal and entitled to respect — because all people are made in the image of God.

"So God created man in his own image, in the image of God he created him; male and female he created them." Genesis 1:27

"You, my brothers, were called to be free. But do not use your freedom to indulge the sinful nature; rather, serve one another in love." Galatians 5:13

2) Everyone is free — to think and to choose how to behave (although Christians hope people will choose to live in love)

Protestant ministers were heavily involved in the drafting of the Universal Declaration of Human Rights.

The Government and Charities Protect People's Rights

1) The Government provides all UK citizens with free healthcare, free education up to the age of 18 and support to help find a home or job (the welfare system). Charities like Barnardo's and Shelter are also there to help people stay alive and healthy if they fall through the gaps in the system.

2) But other rights, such as freedom of opinion, freedom of expression and freedom from imprisonment, aren't universal. The Government will limit these rights if they think it's for the good of the community, e.g. you're not allowed to say anything that might encourage racial or religious hatred, and terrorism suspects can be held for up to 28 days without charge.

3) Human rights charities, like Amnesty International and Liberty, constantly challenge these decisions to limit people's rights. They argue that any limitations on freedom of speech are dangerous, since they can restrict debate on important issues.

You've gotta fight... for your right... to RE...

Some governments don't agree with the idea of human rights. They argue that the UN declaration was written by Western countries, reflecting Western values — so it isn't always appropriate for non-Western countries.

Democracy

Whether you're interested in politics or not, you can't get away from how <u>important</u> it is and how much it affects <u>everyone's</u> lives — yours included. In fact, it's <u>so</u> important that they've put it on the Religious Studies syllabus... well, obviously... the connection's quite clear... ahem...

Democracy *is 'Rule by the People'*

1) The UK is a <u>democratic society</u> — the <u>people</u> select <u>representatives</u> (e.g. MPs) to run the country.
2) We <u>elect</u> MPs to form a government every five years or so. If a government makes lots of unpopular decisions, they can be kicked out at the next general election. This helps keep their power in <u>check</u>.
3) But democracy is about <u>more</u> than voting — in a democratic society, people can speak out, or take part in <u>peaceful protest</u> if they want something changed.

Democratic Processes **are Important**

A <u>democratic process</u> is <u>any</u> way in which citizens can take part in the running of a country:

- <u>VOTING</u> — This is the most <u>obvious</u> way to affect government. UK citizens can be asked to vote for a <u>representative</u> (e.g. in local council, general or European elections) or on a particular issue in a <u>referendum</u>. A referendum is a "yes" or "no" vote on a question that's considered <u>too important</u> to be decided by representatives, e.g. the UK joining the Euro.

- <u>PROTESTING</u> for or against a government decision — This can take many forms, e.g. <u>writing</u> to your representative, signing a written <u>petition</u> or taking part in a <u>protest march</u>.

- Joining a <u>PRESSURE GROUP</u> — These organisations try to <u>influence</u> government decisions on particular issues, e.g. <u>Greenpeace</u> or the <u>Stop the War Coalition</u>.

- Joining a <u>POLITICAL PARTY</u> — Political parties are groups of (usually) <u>like-minded</u> people who try to get elected based on <u>policies</u>. There are three main parties in the UK — Labour, the Conservatives and the Liberal Democrats. Party members can stand as <u>candidates</u> for election, <u>campaign</u> on behalf of a candidate or just <u>donate money</u> to help pay for election campaigns.

It's <u>really important</u> to take part in these processes, because they give you a <u>say</u> in how the country's run. Decisions that affect <u>your lives</u> are being made <u>every day</u> by the people in power. Democratic processes let you make your <u>opinions</u> known, to help you influence those <u>decisions</u>.

Democracy can bring about real <u>social change</u> — changes in the structure, behaviour and attitudes of society (for better or for worse). And that affects everyone, so make sure you have a voice.

Electoral Processes — *Organising the Voting System*

1) In the UK, <u>every citizen over 18</u> has the right to vote (unless they're in prison).
2) Voting happens at a <u>polling station</u> — somewhere local with easy access, such as a village hall. Voting is secret so it's fair — you're not bullied into voting for one particular candidate.
3) There are two electoral <u>systems</u> used in the UK:

First-past-the-post: This is the system used in most UK elections. The country is divided into voting areas called <u>constituencies</u> (for general elections) and <u>wards</u> (for local elections). The candidate with the most votes in each constituency or ward is elected to represent that area.

Proportional representation: This is only used in European elections, and in elections to the Northern Irish, Scottish and Welsh assemblies. Each person votes for a <u>political party</u>. The number of representatives elected from that party is <u>proportional</u> to the total number of votes they got.

Democracy — *power to the people...*

Yeah, yeah, politics — how dull, yawn. But free and fair elections and the right to peaceful protest are vital parts of our society, and they should never be taken for granted. Once you get the vote — use it wisely.

Christian Teachings on Responsibility

Christians believe that they have a <u>responsibility</u> to care for other people.

The Golden Rule — a Moral Rule of Thumb

Christian moral teachings on <u>duty</u> and <u>responsibility</u> come down to this one basic rule:

> "So in everything, do to others what you would have them
> do to you, for this sums up the Law and the Prophets." Matthew 7:12

1) That means Christians should always think about <u>others</u>, not just themselves.

2) It's the same sort of vibe as *"love your neighbour as yourself"* (Leviticus 19:18). But Christians have a <u>responsibility</u> to put this love into <u>practice</u>, e.g. by offering support, shelter, food or clothing to someone in need.

Most Christian denominatio remind people to "<u>Go out to love and serve the Lord</u>" at th end of a service.

The Sheep and the Goats is a Parable of Judgement Day

1) In the Gospel of Matthew (Matthew 25:31-46), Jesus tells a story about the <u>end of the world</u> and how everyone will be judged and separated into the <u>good</u> (the <u>sheep</u>) and the <u>bad</u> (the <u>goats</u>).

> "He will put the sheep on his right and the goats on his left.
> Then the King will say to those on his right, 'Come, you who are blessed by my Father...
> For I was <u>hungry</u> and you gave me something to eat, I was <u>thirsty</u> and you gave me something to drink, I was a <u>stranger</u> and you invited me in, I needed <u>clothes</u> and you clothed me, I was <u>sick</u> and you looked after me, I was in <u>prison</u> and you came to visit me.'" Matthew 25:33-36

2) But the people <u>won't remember</u> helping Jesus (and let's face it — it's not the sort of thing you'd forget)...

> The King will reply, 'I tell you the truth, whatever you did for one of the <u>least of these brothers of mine</u>, you did for <u>me</u>.'
> Then he will say to those on his left, 'Depart from me, you who are cursed, into the eternal fire...
> ...whatever you did <u>not</u> do for one of the least of these, you did not do for me.'" Matthew 25:40-41 & 45

3) Jesus is saying that helping <u>any other person</u> is just as <u>good</u> as helping him. And that if you <u>don't</u> help a starving person, it's <u>as bad</u> as leaving Jesus hungry.

Genesis 4:1-10 — "Am I my Brother's Keeper?"

1) Genesis 4:1-10 is the story of the brothers <u>Cain and Abel</u>.

2) Cain commits <u>three sins</u>: i) he's <u>jealous</u> of his brother Abel; ii) he acts on his jealousy by <u>killing</u> Abel; iii) then he <u>lies</u> to God about it.

3) When God asks Cain where Abel is, he replies: *"I don't know... <u>Am I my brother's keeper?</u>"*

4) The story of Cain is referred to later, in the <u>New Testament</u>, where Cain represents those without love for others. This quote is from the <u>first letter of John</u>.

5) John is saying that it's not enough to go around <u>talking</u> about love and charity and <u>claiming</u> to be Christian. A true Christian <u>acts</u> to help people who need it.

> "...We should <u>love</u> one another. Do not be like Cain, who belonged to the evil one and murdered his brother... We know that we have passed from death to life, because we love our brothers...
> This is how we know what love is: Jesus Christ laid down his life for us. And we ought to lay down our lives for our brothers. If anyone has material possessions and sees his brother in need but has no pity on him, how can the love of God be in him?
> Dear children, <u>let us not love with words or tongue but with actions and in truth</u>." 1 John 3: 11-18

This should sort the sheep from the goats...

Lots of Bible quotes here. For "The Sheep and the Goats" and "Cain and Abel", you need to go away and read the full excerpts — there isn't room to put the whole lot on this page. The main point here is that, for Christians, it's not enough just to <u>feel sorry</u> for people — they have a <u>duty</u> to actively <u>help</u> people.

Genetic Engineering

Scientific advances mean we can now alter the genes of any living thing to try to get the features we want. But just because we can, that doesn't necessarily mean we should...

You Need to Know about Genetic Engineering and Cloning

There are ethical issues involved with lots of different biotechnologies.
The two you need to know about are:

> GENETIC ENGINEERING — manipulating genes, e.g. moving genes from one organism to another to make an organism with more useful features.   Bacteria can be engineered to produce human insulin for people with diabetes, and crop plants can be made more nutritious or more resistant to disease.
>
> CLONING — producing offspring that are genetically identical to the parent.

1) These technologies have the potential to solve many problems (e.g. helping treat diseases or making food production more efficient).
2) Genetic engineering could be used to create an organism (e.g. a crop plant) with all the right characteristics, then that organism could be cloned to produce as many copies of it as we need.
3) For example, genetically modifying crop plants to increase the nutritional value and yield could mean we can produce more than enough food for everyone.
4) Animals can be engineered to produce medicines in their milk to treat diseases.
5) But not everyone thinks it's such a great idea...

There are Practical Issues with Biotechnology...

Some people disagree with genetic engineering and cloning for practical reasons:
1) Creating very successful crop plants is likely to affect the number and variety of weeds living in and around the crops. This could reduce biodiversity.
2) Not everyone is convinced that genetically modified crops or farm animals will be safe to eat.
3) There's a risk that transplanted genes could get out into the natural environment — e.g. herbicide resistance could be picked up by wild plants, creating 'superweeds'.
4) Some people feel that we don't understand genes well enough to know the full effects of tampering with them. Transplanting a gene could create unforeseen problems.
5) Cloning has the problem of reducing the gene pool. Lots of copies of the same organism mean fewer different genes in the population. That leaves the population more susceptible to disease.
6) Also, cloning animals is a difficult process — embryos formed by cloning often don't develop properly, and the adults produced tend to suffer health problems and die young.

I probably shouldn't be

"I have created the perfect beast!! Mwah ha ha ha..."

...as well as Purely Moral Ones

1) Some people think it's wrong to change the characteristics of an organism purely for human benefit.
2) Others worry that we won't stop at engineering plants and animals. That those who can afford it might decide which characteristics they want their children to have, creating a 'genetic underclass'.
3) Therapeutic cloning means creating an embryo that's a clone of an ill person, then taking stem cells from it to grow new organs. This destroys the embryo, which some Christians feel denies the sanctity of life.
4) Other Christians worry that any clone who lived to adulthood wouldn't have a soul.
5) Many Roman Catholics and other Christians are completely opposed to genetic engineering and cloning — they see them as 'playing God'. Christianity teaches that all creation belongs to God, so by creating new organisms ourselves, some Christians believe we're trying to step into God's shoes.

My mate played God in a play once — I was a sheep...

Cloning humans has the added ethical question of why someone's doing it. Some people might want to achieve immortality that way. But of course, the clone wouldn't be them — it would be like an identical twin.

Practice Questions

This is all really fundamental stuff. This section is about what's <u>right</u> and what's <u>wrong</u>. It's about the way <u>all</u> human beings should expect to be treated — for no better reason than that they're human.
Deep.

But what it's <u>also</u> about is getting you through the 'Rights and Responsibilities' bit of your exam. And that's where these questions come in. If there are any you can't answer, go back and look at the relevant pages, then try again. There's a glossary at the back to help you with the 'definitions' questions, and pages 29-31 have plenty of tips for answering the wordy ones.

1) What is:
   a) the Bible?
   b) conscience?
   c) the Decalogue?
   d) Situation Ethics?
   e) a human right?
   f) a democratic process?
   g) a political party?
   h) a pressure group?
   i) social change?
   j) the Golden Rule?

   These "definition" questions are worth 2 marks each in the exam, so make sure you give a <u>full</u> definition.

2) For each of the following questions, give <u>two</u> reasons for your point of view.
   a) Do you think you should trust your conscience?
   b) Do you think human rights are important?
   c) Do you think freedom of speech is important?
   d) Do you think genetic engineering should be used to create better crops?

   These questions aren't asking for a balanced argument, just two good reasons for <u>one</u> opinion. Each reason's worth 2 marks in the exam.

3) For these questions, take extra care with your spelling, punctuation and grammar, and express yourself as clearly as possible.
   a) Explain why some Christians use only the Bible as a basis for making moral decisions.
   b) Explain why some Christians use Situation Ethics as a basis for making moral decisions.
   c) Explain how pressure groups and political parties can help to bring about social change.
   d) Explain how the Parable of the Sheep and the Goats illustrates Christian teachings on responsibility.
   e) Explain why some Christians are in favour of the use of genetic engineering and some are not.

   "Explain" means you have to say <u>why</u>, not just <u>what</u> people believe. These questions test your 'clarity of expression' as well as what you know. They're worth 8 marks each in the exam, so they're important.

4) Read the following statements:
   a) "Christians should base their moral decisions entirely on the teachings of the Church."
   b) "All Christians should support human rights."
   c) "It is important to take part in democratic processes."
   d) "Christians have a duty to care for other people."
   For each statement:
   (i) Do you agree? Give reasons for your opinion.
   (ii) Give reasons why some people may disagree with you.
   In your answers you should refer to Christianity.

   More <u>opinion</u> questions — worth 3 marks for <u>each</u> side of the argument. But this time, you have to give some <u>religious</u> views in your answer. If you don't refer to Christianity in at least one part of the question you lose <u>half</u> the marks, straight off.

Global Warming

The Earth suffers from many environmental problems. Sadly, most of these problems are man-made...

Global Warming — the Planet is Heating Up

1) There are several gases in the atmosphere that help keep the Earth warm.
They're called "greenhouse gases" and the main ones are carbon dioxide and methane.

2) Over the past century, the amount of greenhouse gases in the atmosphere has increased,
and measurements show that the Earth has got hotter. This effect is called global warming.

3) There's now a consensus among climate scientists that the increasing levels of greenhouse
gases have caused most of the increase in temperature.

4) There are still a few scientists around who don't agree with the consensus view. They argue
that the recent warming either isn't significant, or can be explained by natural effects.

Global Warming Could Lead to Very Serious Problems

Nobody knows for sure what'll happen if the Earth keeps getting hotter.
But if climate scientists are right, there are plenty of reasons to be worried about global warming:

- The increase in air temperature will make the sea warmer. As the sea heats up
it will expand, causing sea levels to rise, which could flood low-lying places.

- Higher temperatures make ice melt. Water that's currently 'trapped' on
land (as ice) could run into the sea, causing sea levels to rise even more.

- Weather patterns could be affected (climate change),
leading to more hurricanes, droughts and floods. As a result:
  - plant species could die out,
  - animal species might have to migrate (bringing them into competition
with humans for food and territory) or might die out completely,
  - fertile land for growing food could be flooded or turn into desert,
  - millions of people could be forced to move.

Solving the Problem is Really Hard

1) Greenhouse gases are released into the atmosphere by various human activities,
e.g. burning fossil fuels for electricity and transport, felling trees and rearing cattle.

2) By agreeing to cut down on these activities, e.g. through treaties like the Kyoto Protocol,
governments hope to reduce greenhouse gas emissions and prevent climate change.
But it's almost impossible to set worldwide targets.

3) Some governments look to short-term benefits, rather than long-term care for
the planet. They may say they're trying to do the best for their people, and that
people should be our first priority.

4) Competition means that businesses often feel forced to put profit before the
welfare of the planet — if they don't, they may not survive.

5) And developed countries are the worst, but not the only polluters. Governments
of developing nations often claim they're only doing now what richer countries
did in the past, and that it's hypocritical for richer countries to tell them not to.

And global warming isn't all we've got to worry about — there's more over the page...

If you've ever fancied seeing the Maldives — do it soon...

You'd be forgiven for thinking you'd stumbled into a science book by mistake (aarrghhh!!!). In fact, you're
probably wondering what on earth any of this has to do with Religious Studies. Well, you need to know
about the issues before you can learn how religious people react to them. Fret not, all will be revealed...

More Environmental Threats

Humans have come up with <u>all sorts</u> of ways of damaging the environment...

Our <u>surroundings</u>, that we <u>depend on</u> for survival.

We Produce Lots of Different Pollutants

In Water

1) <u>Sewage</u>, <u>agricultural chemicals</u> (e.g. fertilisers) and <u>toxic chemicals</u> from industry can pollute lakes, rivers and oceans.

2) These pollutants <u>harm</u> the plants and animals that live in and around the water, including humans.

3) In many countries, there are now <u>tight restrictions</u> on the types and amounts of chemicals that can be released into waterways, although <u>accidental spills</u> still happen (e.g. oil spills at sea).

On Land

1) We use <u>toxic chemicals</u> for farming (e.g. pesticides and herbicides), although many farms are moving towards <u>organic</u> solutions, which are less damaging.

2) We also bury <u>nuclear waste</u> underground, and we dump a lot of <u>household</u> and <u>industrial waste</u> in landfill sites. These toxic chemicals can <u>kill</u> plants and animals, and cause <u>cancer</u> in humans.

In the Air

1) <u>Smoke</u> and <u>gases</u> from vehicles and industry can pollute the air, e.g.:
   - <u>Sulfur dioxide</u> and <u>nitrogen oxides</u> can cause <u>acid rain</u>.
   - Fine dust called '<u>particulates</u>' can cause health problems in humans.
   - <u>CFCs</u> damage the ozone layer.

2) Most of these pollutants can now be <u>removed</u> from waste gases before they reach the atmosphere (but that doesn't mean they always are).

And We're Running Out of Natural Resources

1) The Earth's population is <u>increasing</u> — it has more than <u>doubled</u> in the last 50 years.

2) At the same time, our <u>standard of living</u> is improving — particularly in developing nations.

3) Combining these two factors means we use more <u>raw materials</u> and more <u>energy</u> for manufacturing processes every year. If we carry on as we are, these natural resources will eventually <u>run out</u>.

4) One solution is to <u>recycle</u>. There are several advantages to recycling:

   - There's a <u>finite</u> amount of natural resources (e.g. metals, oil for fuel and plastics) in the Earth. Recycling <u>conserves</u> them.

   - <u>Mining</u>, <u>extracting</u> and <u>making</u> materials (e.g. metals or glass) needs lots of <u>energy</u>, which mostly comes from burning <u>fossil fuels</u>. Fossil fuels are expensive, will run out one day, and cause pollution. Recycling things like copper, aluminium and glass takes much <u>less energy</u> (although this isn't true for all materials).

   - Recycling also cuts down on the amount of <u>rubbish</u> that goes to landfill, which takes up space and pollutes the surroundings.

5) <u>Fertile land</u> for growing crops is another natural resource that's in danger of running out. Every year, overgrazing and irresponsible farming methods turn more fertile land into <u>desert</u>.

A <u>natural resource</u> is just anything found naturally that's useful to humans.

<u>Conservation</u> means protecting and preserving things, particularly natural resources.

Simon didn't see why land being turned into dessert was such a bad thing...

More people, more mess, fewer resources...

Uuurghhh... it's all a bit depressing isn't it. But I suppose that's what you get for choosing a unit called "Religion and Society". It's that "Society" bit... dead giveaway (what do you mean, 'I'm a cynic' — youth of today...) Anyway — make sure you've got all the issues firmly embedded in your noggin, then you can put your RS hat back on. You're about to find out the religious take on all this...

Stewardship

Christianity, Islam and Judaism have pretty underlined ideas when it comes to looking after the Earth. They teach that God has put us in charge of the Earth, but that we must do our duty responsibly.

Religious Ideas about the Environment — 'Stewardship'

CHRISTIANITY

1) Christians of all denominations believe that the Earth is God's creation. They believe that God gave us the Earth, but expects us to care for it — this idea is called 'stewardship'. We have no right to abuse God's creation, but must act responsibly.

2) There's pressure on governments and companies to sell goods and services, even at the expense of the environment. Although it can be difficult to balance taking care of the Earth with providing for humankind, this is what Christians believe we must try to do.

> "We have a responsibility to create a balanced policy between consumption and conservation." Pope John Paul II, 1988

3) Christianity teaches that everything is interdependent (i.e. everything depends on everything else), so driving species of animal or plant to extinction, or harming the planet, eventually ends up harming us.

4) Christian organisations such as CAFOD, Christian Aid and Tearfund® are concerned with putting this responsibility into practice. They put pressure on governments and industry to think more about how we are abusing the planet.

> "You made him [humankind] a little lower than the heavenly beings, and crowned him with glory and honour. You made him ruler over the works of your hands; you put everything under his feet." Psalm 8:5-6

> "The earth is the Lord's, and everything in it, the world and all who live in it; for he founded it upon the seas and established it upon the waters." Psalm 24:1-2

JUDAISM

1) Jews believe that we are the custodians of the Earth, and a concern for the natural world is often seen as being at the heart of Jewish teaching.

2) God's creations should remain as he intended, and we have no right to abuse them. Everything is interdependent, with trees being particularly important. Since the creation of Israel in 1948, millions of trees have been planted to aid the reclamation of the desert and help rebuild the nation.

> "The Lord God took the man and put him in the Garden of Eden, to work it and take care of it." Genesis 2:15

ISLAM

1) Muslim teaching on environmental issues is very similar to that of Judaism.

2) At the Day of Judgement questions will be asked of us. We will be required to answer for any ill-treatment of the planet and its resources.

3) The Earth is seen as being a product of the love of Allah, so we should treat it with love.

> Dr Abdullah Omar Nasseef stated at the 1996 World Wide Fund for Nature conference that, "His [Allah's] trustees are responsible for maintaining the unity of his creation, the integrity of the Earth, its flora and fauna, its wildlife and natural environment."

Look after the planet — or it's eternal damnation, my friend...

Once again, the ideas of all three of these religions are very similar. Which is good for me, since I don't have to write as much. And good for you, since you don't have to remember as much — even if you're studying all of these religions. If you're just studying two of them, then you've got it easy anyway, I reckon.

Infertility Treatment

There are many <u>similarities</u> in the opinions of Christians, Muslims and Jews towards infertility treatment. All believe that a child is a <u>gift</u>, and so all allow <u>some</u> methods of infertility treatment. But before you get into the details of what religions teach, you need to know a bit about the different <u>treatment options</u>. (And that means some science again, I'm afraid.)

<u>Infertility</u> means an Inability to <u>Conceive</u> a Child

1) If a couple is '<u>infertile</u>', it means they can't have <u>children</u> together.

2) There are <u>many reasons</u> for infertility. Some of the common ones are:
   - the woman isn't producing <u>eggs</u>,
   - the man doesn't have enough <u>sperm</u> (called a 'low sperm count'),
   - the man's sperm are <u>damaged</u> in some way,
   - the woman's eggs aren't getting to the <u>womb</u> properly,
   - the woman can't <u>carry</u> a pregnancy to term, e.g. she becomes pregnant but miscarries.

3) Nowadays, there are various kinds of <u>infertility treatment</u> that can be used to help. Which treatments are likely to work depends on what's causing the infertility.

<u>Artificial Insemination</u> is Often the <u>First Step</u>

1) If eggs are getting to the woman's womb, this is often the <u>first thing</u> doctors try.

2) Sperm are <u>injected</u> directly into the woman's <u>womb</u>. It's timed so that the sperm is injected at about the <u>same time</u> as the egg is arriving from her ovary.

3) There are <u>two</u> types of artificial insemination:

> <u>Artificial Insemination by the Husband</u> (<u>AIH</u>) — sperm from the <u>husband</u> is injected into the wife's womb. This is the most common type, and helps if the problem is to do with the number or activity of sperm.
>
> <u>Artificial Insemination by Donor</u> (<u>AID</u>) — sperm from a <u>sperm bank</u> (i.e. an anonymous donor) is used. This is only used if the husband's sperm is too badly damaged to fertilise an egg. IVF with the husband's sperm is usually tried first (see below).

IVF — In-Vitro <u>Fertilisation</u>

1) In <u>in-vitro fertilisation</u>, eggs and sperm are mixed in a <u>test-tube</u>.

2) Often, this process results in <u>several embryos</u> — either one or two of which are <u>implanted</u> into the woman's womb.

> An <u>embryo</u> is a fertilised egg in the first eight weeks after fertilisation. In Britain, any <u>extra</u> embryos can legally be used in <u>experiments</u> until they are 14 days old — at this time they must be <u>destroyed</u>.

3) Depending on the <u>cause</u> of the infertility, IVF could involve:

> <u>Egg Donation</u> — when an egg from a <u>different</u> woman is used. This is necessary if the wife can't produce healthy eggs.
>
> <u>Sperm Donation</u> — when sperm from a <u>sperm bank</u> is used.
>
> <u>Surrogacy</u> — when a different woman <u>bears</u> the child for the couple. A surrogate mother is needed if the wife can't carry a pregnancy to term. Surrogacy doesn't <u>have</u> to involve IVF, but it often does — so that the child is biologically related to both the husband and wife, rather than to the surrogate. The alternative is to <u>artificially inseminate</u> the surrogate with the husband's sperm.

<u>No — fertiliser won't help...</u>

All the way through this page, I've referred to the couple as 'husband' and 'wife' — but that's just shorthand really. In the UK, all young women are entitled to infertility treatment, so long as they're in a position to offer 'supportive parenting' — that is, they have to be in a stable relationship (heterosexual or homosexual).

Infertility Treatment: Religious Views

So, infertility treatment can involve just the couple (with a bit of help from the people in the white coats), or it could involve egg and sperm donors too.

In general, religious teachings only allow for the use of reproductive technology for heterosexual married couples, since marriage is seen as the proper context for raising children by all three faiths.

Christianity sees Children as a Blessing from God

1) Most Christian Churches believe that it's okay for science to help childless couples to conceive — as long as the process doesn't involve anyone else.

2) For this reason, artificial insemination using the husband's sperm (AIH) is permissible. The couple can be blessed with a child — and as no 'third party' is involved, the sanctity of marriage is not interfered with. Many Roman Catholics still aren't keen though, since the sperm comes from an 'unnatural' sex act.

3) For some Christians (particularly in the Roman Catholic Church), AIH is as far as a childless couple should go with infertility treatment. If it fails, they're encouraged to adopt instead. Though many other Christians consider IVF an appropriate treatment if the wife's egg and husband's sperm are used.

4) Artificial insemination using donated sperm (AID) is a much less favoured method, as the sperm is not that of the husband. Likewise, the use of a different woman's egg — either as part of a surrogacy arrangement or in IVF egg donation.

5) The Roman Catholic Church is opposed to IVF in all forms, as it often leads to the creation of 'spare' embryos. These can be used for experimentation or simply thrown away. Many Catholics argue that life begins at fertilisation, and that even an embryo has rights.

Muslim Views are along the Same Lines

1) Again, scientific methods are permissible — as long as no 'third party' is involved, and all other natural methods of conceiving have failed.

2) Artificial insemination and IVF are both believed to be reasonable, as long as the egg of the wife and the sperm of the husband are used.

3) However, AID is not acceptable as the sperm is donated. Many Muslims see this as a sin comparable with adultery, as the woman has become pregnant using the sperm of a man other than her husband.

4) There are also concerns about diseases that could be inherited from an anonymous sperm donor (although most sperm banks screen donors for serious genetic disorders).

5) Shi'ite Muslims sometimes allow egg donation, so long as the donor is a Muslim woman, and there is no other way for the couple to have a child.

Jewish Attitudes are Similar too

Louise hoped that the 'lemon look' would catch on.

1) In Jewish teaching, there's an emphasis on having a family.

> "Be fruitful and increase in number; fill the earth..."
> Genesis 1:28

2) Because of this, it's left to individual married couples to decide whether they need to turn to scientific methods of conception.

3) A Jewish couple might seek advice on the matter from their rabbi (religious leader).

4) AIH is usually permitted, but not AID, as the use of donated sperm might be seen as a form of adultery.

5) IVF is generally approved of — as long as the egg and the sperm are from the married couple involved.

6) Egg donation is seen as okay, though the couple will often prefer the egg to come from a Jewish woman. This is because, according to Orthodox teachings, you're only a Jew if your mother is a Jew.

For many couples, adoption isn't enough...

Not being able to have children can be heartbreaking for a couple. If the technology exists to help them have a child, but their religion is against using it, what should they do... tricky. If you know people with personal experience in this area, you could use that in the exam to put the religious view in perspective.

Transplant Surgery

Transplant surgery is fairly commonplace nowadays. A lot of people carry a donor card
(which says they'd like their organs to be donated to someone else after they die).

Transplant Surgery can Save Lives

1) Transplant surgery is the replacement of a faulty organ with a healthy one.
2) Transplants can be used to replace organs that have been damaged. They can also be used to cure disorders like leukaemia (with a bone marrow transplant) and diabetes (with a pancreas transplant).
3) Some organs, e.g. kidneys (which we've got two of) and bone marrow (which we can replace) can be donated from living donors. But most organs, e.g. heart, liver, pancreas, eyes, etc. can only be transplanted shortly after the death of the donor.
4) There's a worldwide shortage of organs for transplantation, though, so about 60% of all patients waiting for a transplant die on the waiting list.

Most Christians are in Favour of Organ Donation

Many Christian organisations encourage organ donation, but not all Christians feel the same way:

ARGUMENTS FOR ORGAN DONATION
- Christians have a duty to help and care for others.
- Donating your organs (before or after death) to save a life is an act of Christian love and charity.
- Most Christians believe God won't need bodies to be intact to resurrect them at Judgement Day, so there's no harm in donating organs after death.

ARGUMENTS AGAINST ORGAN DONATION
- The human body is sacred and so shouldn't be tampered with after death.
- As a living donor, you put your own life at risk.
- Family members can feel pressurised to allow a loved-one's organs to be donated.
- Transplants could encourage harvesting and sale of organs from developing countries.

The Jehovah's Witnesses used to ban their members from receiving transplants, because they saw it as cannibalism. Transplants are now allowed, so long as the organ is completely drained of blood.

Saving Life is Very Important to Jews and Muslims

JEWISH VIEWS
1) Jews believe that the human body is sacred, so it's usually forbidden to mutilate a body, e.g. remove organs.
2) It is also forbidden to benefit from a corpse.
3) But most rabbis are prepared to overrule these objections to save a life.
4) For Orthodox Jews, this usually means organ donation is allowed if there's a specific person who needs the organ right then. Reform Jews will also allow organs to be taken where there isn't a known recipient yet.
5) In all cases, it has to be very clear that the donor is actually dead, beyond resuscitation (i.e. brain dead), before the organs can be taken. The organs must be removed respectfully, with the minimum damage to the body.

MUSLIM VIEWS
1) Muslims have very similar views to Jews about the sanctity of the human body, and the respect that it should be shown. Some Muslims also believe that human organs belong to Allah, so we have no right to give them away.
2) Others argue that, according to Shari'ah (Islamic law), even some forbidden things are allowed when the alternative is death. They also argue that you should always choose the lesser of two evils.

"...But whoever is forced [by necessity], neither desiring [it] nor transgressing [its limit], there is no sin upon him. Indeed, Allah is Forgiving and Merciful." Qur'an 2:173

Save a life — carry a donor card...

A couple of techniques in the pipeline are xenotransplantation (using genetically modified animal organs) and growing organs in the lab. In the future, these methods could solve the organ shortage problem for good, and get rid of the need to take organs from other humans. But they have medical and ethical issues of their own...

Practice Questions

I bet you thought Religious Studies was all about God and churches and stuff. Little did you know that you'd be learning about environmental issues, infertility and organ donation. But RS is all about things that affect people. So lucky, lucky you... you get to learn about all this malarkey.

But just to check that you've learnt all you need to know, have a go at these questions. You'll probably be brilliant at them (well, you might be, anyway). But if there are any you can't answer, go back and check out the relevant bit of the section, and then have another go at the questions.

1) What is:
   a) global warming?
   b) the environment?
   c) a natural resource?
   d) conservation?
   e) stewardship?
   f) infertility?
   g) artificial insemination?
   h) in-vitro fertilisation?
   i) surrogacy?
   j) organ donation?

If you learn your definitions, these are 2 easy marks in the exam. Try the glossary at the back of the book if you're struggling.

2) For each of the following questions, give two reasons for your point of view.
   a) Do you think we should reduce our greenhouse gas emissions?
   b) Do you think it's important to conserve natural resources?
   c) Do you agree with the use of donor sperm to help a childless couple conceive?
   d) Do you agree with organ transplants?

These questions are asking for your opinion as well as reasons to back it up. These questions are worth 4 marks each, so you have to give detailed reasons.

3) For these questions, take extra care with your spelling, punctuation and grammar, and express yourself as clearly as possible.
   a) Explain what Christians mean by 'stewardship'.
   b) Choose one religion other than Christianity and explain its teachings on environmental issues.
   c) Explain why some Christians are in favour of in-vitro fertilisation treatment for infertile couples, and some are not.
   d) Choose one religion other than Christianity and explain its teachings on infertility treatment.
   e) Choose one religion and explain why some of its followers are in favour of organ donation and some are not.

These 8-mark questions can make a big difference to your grade. Have a look at p.30 for some advice on answering them.

4) Read the following statements:
   a) "Global warming is a very serious problem."
   b) "Religious people should treat the planet with respect."
   c) "Religious people should support infertility treatment."
   d) "Religious people should carry a donor card."
   For each statement:
   (i) Do you agree? Give reasons for your opinion.
   (ii) Give reasons why some people may disagree with you.
   In your answers you should refer to at least one religion.

It's 3 marks for one argument and 3 marks for the other. So for each part of the question you need three simple reasons, two detailed reasons or one really in-depth reason. And that means sitting down and learning the arguments properly.

World Peace

World peace — a pretty tall order, but there are a lot of people <u>striving</u> for it...

The <u>United Nations (UN)</u> works for <u>World Peace</u>

1) An organisation called the <u>League of Nations</u> was formed after the First World War to <u>promote peace and cooperation</u> between countries. But the <u>League was ineffective</u> — some major countries didn't join it (e.g. the USA), others joined but then left (e.g. Russia, Germany, Italy, Japan).

2) After World War II <u>the United Nations (UN) replaced the League</u>. Founding members of the UN included the USA, Russia and most of Europe, making it a more effective <u>world body</u>. The UN now has 192 members — the only fully recognised, independent state that <u>isn't</u> a member is Vatican City. (Kosovo, Palestine and Taiwan aren't members, but that's because not everyone recognises them as countries.)

The UN flag

3) The UN works to find <u>peaceful solutions</u> to disputes, to encourage <u>global cooperation</u> on law, security and economic development and to protect people's basic <u>human rights</u>.

4) Its main function is to promote <u>WORLD PEACE</u> — an end to <u>all wars</u>, all over the world.

5) If a country breaks the rules, the UN can impose <u>economic sanctions</u> (stop people trading with them) and send in <u>peacekeeping troops</u>.

UN Peacekeeping and Conflict Resolution

1) A lot of the UN's work is in <u>conflict resolution</u> — ending wars in a way that leads to <u>lasting peace</u>.

2) That means that any peace treaties have to make <u>good compromises</u> and can take <u>years</u> to be agreed on (e.g. the Israeli-Palestinian peace process). The first step, before any negotiations, is a <u>ceasefire</u> (everyone agrees to stop fighting while the negotiators talk).

3) It's the job of <u>UN Peacekeepers</u> to make sure both sides <u>stick</u> to the ceasefire, to <u>protect</u> aid workers and civilians, and to help people <u>rebuild</u>. The UN currently has about <u>15</u> peacekeeping missions in progress, including those in Kosovo, Darfur and the Democratic Republic of the Congo.

There are <u>Religious</u> Peace Organisations Too

There are lots of <u>religious organisations</u> that work outside government to help promote world peace:

PAX CHRISTI — Roman Catholic

Pax Christi is an international, non-profit organisation working for <u>human rights</u>, <u>disarmament</u>, <u>reconciliation</u> (see page 21) and <u>peaceful</u> conflict resolution. For example, they are currently calling for the protection of civilians from fighting in the Democratic Republic of the Congo.

JEWISH PEACE FELLOWSHIP — Jewish

The JPF is a pacifist organisation (see page 18), originally founded to help imprisoned <u>conscientious objectors</u> in World War II. A conscientious objector is someone who refuses to fight because it goes against their beliefs. The organisation believes that military action <u>never</u> solves conflicts, and that <u>active non-violence</u> (e.g. negotiations, promoting social justice) is the only way to settle disputes.

MUSLIM PEACE FELLOWSHIP — Muslim

The Muslim Peace Fellowship is dedicated to making the '<u>beauty of Islam</u>' present in the world. It promotes peace <u>through</u> Islam, and works to bring about changes in society to make it fair and compassionate to <u>all</u> people.

As the great John Lennon said — "I am the walrus"... ...or something

Another organisation worth knowing about is the World Peace Prayer Society. This is a religious organisation, but it doesn't belong to any particular faith. Rather it encourages everyone around the world, whatever their religion, to pray for peace. The prayer is very simple: "May peace prevail on Earth."

The Nature of War

Wars are <u>complex</u> things. They get started for <u>all sorts</u> of reasons — and often it's as much about not being seen to <u>back down</u> as anything more concrete.

Wars can have Many Causes

Most wars have causes that are a <u>combination</u> of loads of different factors, e.g.

<u>Religion:</u> Over the centuries, there have been many wars fought <u>in the name of</u> one religion or another. For example, the Crusades in the 11th, 12th and 13th centuries (see 'Holy War' on the next page). The most obvious modern example of this is the <u>Arab-Israeli war</u>, currently being fought over the holy land of Israel and Palestine.

<u>Defence:</u> '<u>Pre-emptive strikes</u>' are wars started by a country in order to <u>defend</u> itself against future attack. The second Iraq War in 2003 was a good example of this. The US-led Coalition justified the invasion of Iraq as a <u>defensive</u> measure, to protect the rest of the world from <u>weapons of mass destruction</u> (see below).

<u>Tribalism:</u> This tends to trigger what are called '<u>wars of secession</u>', where a group of people within a country fight for their own independent state. It's been at least partly responsible for many civil wars in the 20th century, e.g. in the former Yugoslavia, Rwanda, Burundi and Sudan. <u>Nationalism</u> is a very similar idea.

<u>Honour:</u> Wars are sometimes fought to defend the <u>honour</u> and <u>dignity</u> of a country, or to <u>save face</u>. A recent example of this is the 1982 Falklands War between Argentina and the UK.

> **AGGRESSION** in war means attacking <u>without provocation</u>. An <u>invasion</u> of another country is usually seen as an act of aggression.

<u>Economics:</u> In the past, economic wars tended to be <u>raids</u> (e.g. the <u>Viking</u> raids of medieval England) or <u>invasions</u> to acquire new land and resources (e.g. <u>colonisation</u>). A recent example of this sort of territorial war is the Iraqi invasion of <u>Kuwait</u> in 1990. But this sort of thing doesn't happen much now — since <u>acts of aggression</u> are <u>condemned</u> by the UN.

Economic factors still have an impact on war, just in a more subtle way. <u>Poverty</u> and <u>economic imbalances</u> can mean that people are <u>more likely</u> to feel threatened or dishonoured, or be drawn into tribalism or nationalism.

Unconventional War — WMD and Terrorism

Weapons of mass destruction (WMD) and terrorism could both be described as <u>unconventional</u> warfare.

1) <u>Terrorism</u> is a form of <u>violent protest</u> that goes on all over the world.

2) Terrorists target any <u>person</u>, <u>building</u> or institution that could help their cause. They don't <u>discriminate</u> between civilians and soldiers.

3) A <u>weapon of mass destruction</u> is a weapon that can destroy large areas of land and/or lots of people all at once, e.g. <u>chemical</u>, <u>biological</u> and <u>nuclear</u> weapons. These weapons are also <u>indiscriminate</u>. Chemical and biological weapons are <u>banned</u> by international law — using them is considered a <u>war crime</u>.

4) The Church of England wants countries to reduce the number of nuclear weapons they have. However, it recognises that <u>unilateral disarmament</u> (where just one country gives up its weapons) is a difficult thing for a government to do.

5) That's why it calls for countries to work together and agree on <u>multilateral disarmament</u>, where many countries give up their nuclear arms at the same time.

140 million people died in wars in the 20th century...

Hard to comprehend. It's like wiping out the populations of the UK, France and Australia. For the exam, it's worth learning about a <u>current</u> conflict, especially why it started, and what efforts are being made to end it.

War: Christianity

Although Christianity is generally 'anti-war', many denominations accept that a war can be '<u>just</u>' (i.e. justified). <u>Individuals</u> may not agree with this, however. They may be against war <u>under any circumstances</u>.

There are *Five Conditions* for Declaring a *Just War*

Although Christians recognise that war goes against the teachings of Jesus, most Christian denominations accept that there can be such a thing as a '<u>just war</u>'. According to the current Catechism of the Roman Catholic Church (a sort of religious handbook), a just war should satisfy these <u>conditions</u>:

PROPER AUTHORITY   A war must be declared by a <u>proper authority</u>, e.g. an elected government, a president or a monarch.   *This isn't always listed as a separate point.*

JUST CAUSE   A war must be <u>defensive</u>, preventing damage that would be "*lasting, grave and certain*". This doesn't necessarily mean <u>self-defence</u> — defending a <u>friendly nation</u> or <u>innocent people</u> (e.g. preventing genocide in Rwanda) is also seen as 'just'.
In some versions of 'just war' theory (but not in the Catechism) there's a separate condition of <u>right intention</u>. Even if there <u>is</u> a just cause, that cause mustn't be used as an <u>excuse</u> to achieve an unjust goal — e.g. to punish an enemy or gain land.

LAST RESORT   <u>All</u> other ways of resolving the conflict <u>must</u> have been tried first.

ACHIEVABLE AIM   A war must have a reasonable chance of <u>success</u>. Fighting a war you have <u>no chance</u> of winning is considered a <u>waste</u> of lives.

PROPORTIONALITY   Any harm caused by fighting the war mustn't be <u>as bad</u> as the harm it's trying to prevent. Using <u>weapons of mass destruction</u> (see previous page) would nearly always violate this condition.

> As well as all that, there are conditions for <u>fighting</u> a war justly. These are:
>
> <u>Discrimination</u>: war should <u>discriminate</u> between <u>combatants</u> and <u>civilians</u> — it's not seen as 'just' to deliberately target civilians.
>
> <u>Proportionality</u>: the military <u>advantage</u> gained by an attack must <u>outweigh</u> any harm caused to civilians.

This is different from the 'proportionality' used to <u>justify</u> the war. This is about individual attacks.

Pacifists *and* Martyrs

1) A <u>pacifist</u> is someone who has strongly-held beliefs that war and physical violence are wrong <u>under any circumstances</u>. Pacifists believe that <u>all</u> disputes should be settled <u>peacefully</u>.

2) Some Christians believe that <u>violence</u> goes against Jesus's teachings to love your enemy and 'turn the other cheek' (see page 21).

3) There were pacifists in Britain who refused to fight in the world wars. These '<u>conscientious objectors</u>' went to prison — they were <u>prisoners of conscience</u>. They suffered <u>humiliation</u> in prison, and after they'd been released.

4) <u>Martyrs</u> are prepared to <u>die</u> for their faith. This willingness to sacrifice your own life for what you believe in is fundamental to Christianity and other religions.

5) Many people risk their lives today by preaching the Gospel of Jesus and speaking out against <u>governments</u>

> The <u>Religious Society of Friends</u> (the <u>Quakers</u>) is a Christian denomination that's opposed to war <u>under all circumstances</u>.

> "Put your sword back in its place... for all who draw the sword will die by the sword."
> Matthew 26:52

> A '<u>Holy War</u>' is one where people believe God is 'on their side' — e.g. in the 11th, 12th and 13th centuries, Christians went on <u>crusades</u> to 'free' the Christian holy places in Palestine.

Just war, just cause — just learn it pal...

In the age of weapons of mass destruction, Pope Benedict XVI has questioned whether a 'just war' is possible any more. With these weapons, it's <u>impossible</u> to discriminate between fighters and civilians.

War: Islam and Judaism

Despite the fact that there have been a number of wars between Muslims and Jews, there are many <u>similarities</u> in the way the two religions approach the subject of <u>war</u>.

The <u>Jewish</u> View — <u>Obligatory</u> and <u>Optional</u> Wars

1) The universal greeting amongst Jews is '<u>shalom</u>' (peace) — this is the <u>ideal</u>. War is hated, but there's a belief that war is sometimes <u>necessary</u> to bring about peace.

2) War is divided into two categories — <u>milchemet mitzvah</u> (obligatory war) and <u>milchemet reshut</u> (optional war).

> **The Six-Day War**
>
> In June 1967, Israel launched a series of attacks against its much larger Arab neighbours, destroying the Egyptian Air Force on the ground. After six days' fighting, Israel had won a war against Egypt, Jordan and Syria.

3) An obligatory war might be:
   i) a war fought in <u>self-defence</u>.
   ii) a <u>pre-emptive strike</u> in order to avoid being attacked — the Six-Day War in 1967 for example.
   iii) a war to help neighbouring countries — so that your <u>own</u> country is not invaded.
   iv) a war commanded by <u>God</u>.

4) An <u>optional</u> war should only take place when all attempts to secure peace have <u>failed</u>.

5) No war should be fought to colonise or take <u>revenge</u>. This is <u>forbidden</u>.

The <u>Islamic</u> View — 'Hate Your Enemy Mildly'

Muslims believe that war is sometimes <u>necessary</u>, although the concept of <u>jihad</u> is often misunderstood. These passages sum up Muslim teaching:

> *"He who fights that Allah's Word should be superior, fights in Allah's Cause."*
> **Prophet Muhammad (Sahih Bukhari)**
>
> *"Hate your enemy mildly; he may be your friend one day."* **Ali ibn Abi Talib**

<u>Jihad</u> — there are Two Kinds

1) There are two kinds of <u>jihad</u> (or 'striving')...

   i) a <u>Greater Jihad</u>, which is when a Muslim makes a special effort to be a '<u>pure</u>' Muslim, or fights against his or her own selfish <u>desires</u>.

   ii) a <u>Lesser Jihad</u> — <u>war</u> is an example of a lesser jihad, but it must be fought only as a last resort. These wars are often thought of as '<u>Holy Wars</u>'.

2) Military jihad has very strict <u>rules</u>, and is similar to the Christian idea of a 'just war':
   i) It is justified if it will bring about <u>freedom</u> from tyranny, restore <u>peace</u>, combat <u>oppression</u>, or right <u>injustice</u>.
   ii) It must <u>not</u> be used to colonise, suppress or impose Islam on non-believers.
   iii) The sick, the elderly, women and children should <u>not</u> be harmed, the natural world must not be damaged, and <u>indiscriminate</u> killing should be avoided.
   iv) Jihad must be in the name of <u>Allah</u>, and according to his will. It must be declared by a <u>religious leader</u>, not any old politician.
   v) Dying in the service of Allah turns a Muslim into a <u>martyr</u>. <u>True</u> martyrs go <u>straight</u> to paradise as an <u>instant</u> reward — martyrs don't have to wait for the Day of Judgement.

3) There is no real concept of <u>pacifism</u> in Islam, although <u>peace</u> is always the goal of war.

Peace, love and harmony — seems that's what we all want...

Judaism and Islam seem to have quite a lot <u>in common</u> when you find out a bit more about them. That's true when it comes to war and peace as well. <u>Neither</u> religion believes in unwavering pacifism — the attitude of both religions is that war is sometimes <u>necessary</u>, though always (and inevitably) <u>unpleasant</u>.

Bullying and Family Conflict

Sadly, bullying happens a lot.

Bullying is Exploitation

1) Exploitation means taking advantage of a weaker person or group. And that's what bullying is all about.

2) A bully intimidates, frightens and controls other people that are weaker than them.

3) Acts of bullying can be: physical (e.g. hitting), social (e.g. enforced isolation) or emotional (e.g. verbal abuse, belittling someone or neglect). Bullies often pick on differences like race, religion or disability.

4) All schools have anti-bullying policies. These include:

> - Listening to and supporting the victims of bullying.
> - Dealing with those responsible for the bullying. This usually emphasises counselling and reform (see page 24) rather than punishment. Punishing a bully can just make them resentful, and not change their beliefs or behaviour at all. Many bullies are insecure, and pick on other people to make themselves feel strong.
> - Encouraging everyone in the school to respect other people (to be considerate of other people and their feelings) and to appreciate their differences, to help prevent bullying.

All Religions are Against Bullying

1) Christians, Muslims and Jews believe that all people are created by God, so mistreating another person is mistreating God's creation.

2) In all three faiths, it's a sin to attack someone else without cause — physically or verbally. Judaism specifically forbids spreading nasty rumours about people.

3) All three religions teach that it's important to protect the weak and to free the oppressed.

4) People of all three faiths believe they will answer to God on Judgement Day for harming, or failing to protect, the innocent.

5) Christians also believe that they have a duty to actively care for others (see page 6).

6) St Paul summed up the Christian attitude to bullying in his letter to the Ephesians.

...loose the chains of injustice and untie the cords of the yo[ke] set the oppressed free and break every yoke... Isaiah 58:

"Do not let any unwholesome talk come out of your mouths, but only what is helpful for building others up... Get rid of all bitterness, rage and anger, brawling and slander, along with every form of malice. Be kind and compassionate to one another, forgiving each other, just as in Christ God forgave you." Ephesians 4:29-32

Religion can Cause Conflict within Families

Religion can help to bring families together, but it can also cause conflict. Young people might not want to follow the traditions of their family, particularly in a multicultural, secular (non-religious) country like the UK. Some of the issues that can spark conflict are:

1) SEX/MARRIAGE — this could be sex before marriage, using contraception, homosexuality, marrying outsid[e] the faith, etc. Traditionally, Christianity, Judaism and Islam have had very strict teachings on this sort of thing. They say that sex should be between a man and a woman, inside marriage, and with the intention o[f] having children. Mixed marriages are rarely approved of, since children from them are unlikely to be raised as observant members of either faith.

2) RITUALS/WORSHIP — not keeping religious observances, e.g. community worship, food laws, Shabbat (for Jews). Religious observance is generally declining across the country, particularly amongst the young.

3) TRADITIONS — e.g. arranged marriages and the role of women in the family. Modern equal rights legislation means that women now have all the same opportunities as men. Some daughters of conservativ[e] families want a good education and a career — they don't want to settle down and have children.

Bullies like to feel strong by making you feel weak...

Being bullied can leave you feeling ashamed. But remember, it's never your choice and it's never your fault.

Forgiveness and Reconciliation

Love is all around us — it's everywhere I go. That's good news. But Jesus said forgiveness is also important.

In Christianity Love and Forgiveness go Together

1) Forgiveness means stopping being angry with someone who's done something wrong. Christianity teaches that forgiveness comes from love.

2) Christians believe that Jesus died on the cross to atone for the sins of all those who believed in him, so that God might forgive our sins.

3) Jesus taught that God is always ready to forgive us, but we must accept that forgiveness, and forgive others in turn.

> "For if you forgive men when they sin against you, your heavenly Father will also forgive you. But if you do not forgive men their sins, your Father will not forgive your sins." Matthew 6:14-15

Zacchaeus (Luke 19:1-10)
A story illustrating Jesus putting forgiveness into practice... Jesus goes as a guest to the home of the hated tax collector Zacchaeus, whose life is completely changed after he decides to repent.

4) Forgiveness is closely related to repentance. Christians believe that God's forgiveness can only come when we repent of our sins (i.e. say we are sorry, and turn our backs on them).

5) If we repent, and put our faith in God, God forgives us and we are reconciled with him. Christians believe the same sort of reconciliation (coming together and making peace) is needed between people.

Forgive Your Enemies

> "If someone strikes you on the right cheek, turn to him the other also." Matthew 5:39

1) Jesus taught that people shouldn't seek revenge — he said that they should 'turn the other cheek'.

2) But this doesn't mean being a submissive victim — just that a Christian's response should be based on the principles of love and forgiveness.

3) For example, most Christians believe that if someone commits a crime (anything from petty theft to starting a war), we shouldn't just do nothing. Punishment can be used to reform an offender and to deter others from offending (see page 24).

4) Some people think that it's wrong to keep forgiving people — that if they reoffend they shouldn't be forgiven again (although Jesus said we should forgive *"not seven times, but seventy-seven times"* — Matthew 18:22).

5) There are also some evils that are very hard to forgive. Should we forgive Adolf Hitler or Josef Stalin? Many Christians would say 'yes' — it is better to forgive, for the sake of the forgiver, and leave judgement in the hands of God.

Dick's 'turn the other cheek' philosophy seemed somehow inappropriate, given the circumstances.

> "Anyone who hates his brother is a murderer, and you know that no murderer has eternal life in him." 1 John 3:15

Jews and Muslims have Similar Ideas about Forgiveness

Both Jews and Muslims believe that, just as God is forgiving and merciful towards them, they should forgive other people. They should also seek forgiveness and make atonement for any wrongs they've committed. The Torah and the Qur'an both encourage people to be forgiving and to seek forgiveness.

Specifically Jewish Beliefs About Forgiveness

1) The Medieval rabbi Maimonides wrote in the Mishneh Torah: *"It is forbidden to be obdurate... When asked by an offender for forgiveness, one should forgive with a sincere mind and a willing spirit."*

2) Jews believe that you can only be forgiven by the one you've injured, so God can only forgive a sin against God, not another person. Each year, before Yom Kippur (the Day of Atonement), Jews seek forgiveness from anyone they feel they've hurt during the year.

3) At Yom Kippur, Jews seek God's forgiveness for their sins at the start of the Jewish Year.

Specifically Muslim Beliefs About Forgiveness

1) The Qur'an allows Muslims to seek retribution for injuries, but encourages them to forgive instead: *"And the retribution for an evil act is an evil one like it, but whoever pardons and makes reconciliation — his reward is [due] from Allah..."* Qur'an 42:40

2) Muslims believe that injuries should be forgiven if the offender is sorry and tries to make amends.

3) There are also many Hadith describing the Prophet Muhammad's acts of forgiveness, and other Muslims try to follow his example.

4) The only sin Allah will not forgive is idolatry.

Learn it all — the examiner isn't as forgiving as God...

Members of all faiths believe that there can be no true reconciliation without forgiveness on both sides.

Practice Questions

Weeeeeell... war, death, bullying, families falling apart...
Now that you're all thoroughly depressed, here are some questions to cheer you up again!
You know the drill by now. Try all the questions. If there are any you can't answer, look back at the section, look at the exam help pages at the back, and try the glossary if you're stuck for a definition. Then do those questions again until you're happy with them.

1) What is:
   a) the United Nations?
   b) conflict resolution?
   c) aggression?
   d) a weapon of mass destruction?
   e) pacifism?
   f) bullying?
   g) exploitation?
   h) reconciliation?
   i) forgiveness?

Every question in the exam starts with defining a key term. If you don't learn the definitions (and they're all in the glossary), you're throwing away an easy 2 marks.

2) For each of the following questions, give two reasons for your point of view.
   a) Do you think weapons of mass destruction should ever be used?
   b) Do you think war is always wrong?
   c) Do you think it's important to forgive?

These are pretty big questions, but remember they're only worth 4 marks in the exam. Just state an opinion and give two good reasons for holding it. You don't have to write an essay.

3) For these questions, take extra care with your spelling, punctuation and grammar, and express yourself as clearly as possible.
   a) Explain how one religious organisation works for world peace.
   b) Explain two reasons why wars occur, using examples from recent conflicts.
   c) Explain what Christians mean by a 'just war'.
   d) Explain why some Christians are pacifists and others are not.
   e) Choose one religion other than Christianity and explain its teaching on war.
   f) Explain how religion can lead to conflict within families.
   g) Choose one religion other than Christianity and explain why its followers are opposed to bullying.

These are the big 8-mark ones — so they're worth taking a little bit of time over. And don't forget your spelling, punctuation and grammar.

4) Read the following statements:
   a) "Religion is the best way to achieve world peace."
   b) "Religious people should oppose the use of weapons of mass destruction."
   c) "Religious people should never go to war."
   d) "Religious people should always punish bullies."
   e) "Religious people should always forgive."
   For each statement:
   (i) Do you agree? Give reasons for your opinion.
   (ii) Give reasons why some people may disagree with you.
   In your answers you should refer to at least one religion.

The easiest way to tackle these is to give a secular (non-religious) argument for one part of the question, and a religious counter argument. It doesn't matter which way round you put them, but your arguments have to be detailed enough to get you 3 marks each.

The Need for Law and Justice

Religious beliefs about justice centre around the idea of <u>responsibility</u> — both in terms of <u>answering</u> for the things you do wrong, and of taking responsibility for the care of others.

Law and Justice are Essential to Most Societies

1) Most nations believe that the <u>rule of law</u> is the best way of <u>protecting</u> people in society.

2) Without law there's the risk of <u>chaos</u>. With it, people know what they <u>can</u> and <u>cannot</u> do.

3) <u>Laws</u> are rules made by Parliament and <u>enforced</u> by the courts.

4) Christianity, Islam and Judaism all teach that <u>God</u> has commanded us to follow law. But some religious believers think that <u>religious law</u> is more important than the <u>laws of the land</u>.

5) Where religious law and state law <u>disagree</u> some believers think it's better to commit a <u>crime</u> if it means they avoid committing a <u>sin</u> (see below).

6) <u>Justice</u> is the idea of each person getting what they <u>deserve</u>, and maintaining what's <u>right</u>. In the context of the law, that means making sure the <u>guilty</u> are suitably punished, and that the <u>innocent</u> are protected.

Crime or Sin — State Law versus Religious Law

1) For <u>Christians</u>, there's a difference between a <u>sin</u> and a <u>crime</u>. A sin is when <u>religious</u> law is broken, i.e. when God's teaching is disobeyed. A crime is when the <u>state</u> laws are broken.

2) Christians believe that <u>justice</u> is very important, since we are all <u>equal</u> in the eyes of God. Christians have a <u>duty</u> to look after other people, and try to <u>guide</u> them to do what's right and <u>repent</u> of their sins.

> "Therefore, it is necessary to submit to the authorities, not only because of possible punishment but also because of conscience." Romans 13:5

3) But Jesus taught that <u>judgement</u> and <u>punishment</u> belong to God:

> "Do not judge, or you too will be judged. For in the same way you judge others, you will be judged, and with the measure you use, it will be measured to you." Matthew 7:1-2

Passing judgement on others is seen as <u>hypocrisy</u>.

Muslims Try to Follow Shari'ah

1) <u>Muslims</u> have a clear and detailed religious law (<u>Shari'ah</u>), and this is often the <u>basis</u> for state law in Islamic countries. Saudi Arabia, for example, is run according to this religious law.

2) Muslims believe strongly in <u>justice</u>. The Qur'an teaches that Allah is <u>just</u> and merciful, and that Muslims should treat all people <u>fairly</u> and <u>equally</u>.

3) Muslims consider maintaining justice to be part of their role as 'khalifah' — <u>vice-regents</u> of Allah's creation.

> <u>Muslims</u> believe that Allah sees all. He will know if you have committed a crime and you will be made to answer for it on the <u>Day of Judgement</u>. A truly repentant sinner, however, will be forgiven.

Jewish Laws are Called Mitzvot

> "Appoint judges... and they shall judge the people fairly." Deuteronomy 16:18

1) <u>Judaism</u> teaches that Jews should obey the laws of the land they live in, as well as following the 613 mitzvot (religious laws or commandments) in the Torah.

2) <u>Rabbinical courts</u> (<u>Bet Din</u>) exist in many countries to sort out Jewish disputes.

3) Both in terms of what's <u>due</u> to God, and to fellow Jews, justice is a huge part of Judaism. The Torah is filled with details of <u>laws</u>, <u>rewards</u> and <u>punishments</u>.

Don't pass judgement on others — that's the examiner's job...

For many religious people, justice doesn't have to come in this life, though. Christians, Muslims and Jews all believe that God is a fair judge, and that the guilty will be punished and the good rewarded in the afterlife.

Theories of Punishment

Punishment can be used to 'get back' at someone for committing a crime, or to prevent crime in the future.

The Courts Force Criminals to Take Responsibility

1) The courts pass judgement in cases of law — they decide whether or not someone is guilty of committing a crime, and what punishment they should face if they are guilty.

2) One goal of the court process is to make people take responsibility for their actions, and acknowledge that they owe a 'debt to society'.

3) This 'debt' can be paid in the form of many different punishments. The punishment given will depend on the severity of the crime, whether or not the criminal has broken the law before and whether or not they show repentance (are sorry for what they've done).

REPENT!

Punishment can have Various Aims

There are several different theories of what punishment is for.

Deterrence: The idea that if a punishment is sufficiently bad in some way (e.g. expensive, embarrassing, restricting, painful) it will put people off committing the crime.
This is the idea behind telling people in advance what the punishment for a given crime is — so they understand the consequences.
Critics argue that people don't stop to think about punishment before they commit a crime, especially if they've taken drugs or alcohol, so deterrence doesn't work.

Protection: If a criminal is considered dangerous, this is the idea that their punishment should protect the rest of society, e.g. imprisonment. Not many people would disagree with this, but some would argue that you protect society best by reforming offenders.

Reform: The idea that punishment should aim to change criminals so that they won't reoffend once their punishment is over. This theory is based on the idea that nobody is inherently bad — and that with help, criminals can become useful members of society again. Programmes to help criminals reform include counselling sessions, visiting victims of similar crimes and working in the community.

"Be merciful, just as your Father is merciful." Luke 6:36

Rehabilitation: This is the idea that punishment should prepare the criminal for a return to a normal, useful life. It's closely related to the idea of reform, but a bit more practical. Rehabilitation usually involves the offender improving their education or learning a trade, which helps improve their self-esteem as well as giving them better job prospects.
Some people think this sort of treatment is a waste of money. They argue that criminals will reoffend whatever you do to help them, and that the money would be better spent on hard-working, law-abiding people.

Retribution: Some people think of punishment as a way of taking revenge on a criminal, of making them 'pay' for what they've done.
Critics of this way of thinking argue that revenge doesn't put right the wrong — that it's better to look for a more constructive solution.

"If anyone injures his neighbour... eye for eye, tooth for tooth. As he has injured the other, so he is to be injured." Leviticus 24:19-20

Crime and Punishment — wasn't that set in Russia...

Not for the first time, I'll say that this is a subject with lots of different shades of grey. Should we just lock people up and throw away the key... or is there something else we should be doing... Ho hum, well you should have known that you don't do RS for an easy life. No, sirree... that's why you have General Studies.

Capital Punishment

Capital punishment is <u>killing</u> someone for committing a crime.

There are Lots of Different Ways of Punishing People

1) Punishment can take a variety of forms, including: <u>community service</u>, a <u>fine</u>, <u>probation</u>, a <u>prison</u> sentence, <u>corporal punishment</u> (inflicting pain, e.g. flogging or beating) and <u>capital punishment</u> (death).

2) These different punishments have different <u>aims</u>. For example, <u>fines</u> are designed as <u>deterrents</u>, whereas a <u>prison sentence</u> is primarily to <u>protect society</u>, although most prisons have active reform programmes too.

3) Different countries and religions favour different types of punishment. In general, the punishments given in <u>scripture</u> are fines, corporal punishment or capital punishment.

Capital Punishment Isn't Used Much Nowadays

1) Capital punishment has been used <u>at some time</u> by <u>most</u> societies, for crimes ranging from <u>petty theft</u> to <u>mutiny</u>. Capital punishment has been <u>abolished</u> in many places, including most of Europe and South America. Elsewhere, it only tends to be used for <u>very serious</u> crimes like <u>murder</u>, <u>espionage</u> and <u>treason</u>.

2) There are <u>arguments</u> for and against capital punishment:

FOR CAPITAL PUNISHMENT

- The risk of death might act as a <u>better deterrent</u> to violent criminals than a prison sentence. (Some statistical studies <u>support</u> this view.)
- If you execute a murderer, it's <u>impossible</u> for them to <u>kill again</u>. Imprisoned murderers have been known to <u>order</u> killings from inside jail, or to <u>reoffend</u> when released on parole.

AGAINST CAPITAL PUNISHMENT

- A lot of murders are committed in the heat of the moment (they're not <u>premeditated</u>), so many murderers won't be thinking about the <u>consequences</u> (not an effective deterrent).
- Execution doesn't give the offender the chance to <u>reform</u>.
- There have been cases where someone has been proved <u>innocent after</u> having been executed.

3) There tend to be <u>more</u> murders in countries that <u>use</u> the death penalty than in those that don't. This is often used as an argument against capital punishment, but it's not clear whether one <u>causes</u> the other.

4) Many <u>Christians</u> are opposed to <u>capital punishment</u>, as it doesn't allow for <u>reform</u>, or show <u>mercy</u>. In Matthew 5:38-42, Jesus said that we should set aside *"an eye for an eye"*, in the name of love and forgiveness. However, some Christians in the United States believe that it's a good thing. They say it <u>protects</u> the innocent.

5) The position of the <u>Torah</u> is very clear on the issue. So <u>Judaism</u> will allow execution for murder if the case is absolutely <u>certain</u> (i.e. there are <u>reliable witnesses</u>). Most Jews are in favour of <u>mercy</u>, though.

"If anyone takes the life of a human being, he must be put to death." Leviticus 24:17

The 'Howard League for Penal Reform' was set up by Christians to campaign for punishments that allow offenders to reform.

6) The Qur'an also clearly states the crimes that can be punished by death, but encourages the family of the victim to accept <u>compensation</u> instead.

"...prescribed for you is legal retribution for those murdered — the free for the free, the slave for the slave, and the female for the female. But whoever overlooks from his brother anything, then there should be... payment to him with good conduct. This is an alleviation from your Lord and a mercy..." Qur'an 2:178

For the death penalty to apply in Islam, there must be a <u>confession</u>, or <u>witnesses</u> to the crime.

Wait, wait, he's inno... (bzzzzzz) — oops...

Capital punishment is a very difficult issue for modern religious people. The Bible and Qur'an both say that death is an appropriate punishment for some crimes (have a read of Leviticus chapters 20 and 24 — they're quite scary). But we tend to be a bit more squeamish about killing people these days.

Drugs and Alcohol

Everyone has a <u>view</u> on drugs and drug abuse. But not all drugs are the <u>same</u>.

Most Drugs are Illegal or Age-Restricted

Illegal Drugs: Heroin, Cocaine, Hallucinogens, Cannabis, etc...

1) The <u>Misuse of Drugs Act</u> splits illegal drugs into three categories: Class A (e.g. heroin, cocaine, LSD), Class B (e.g. amphetamines (speed), cannabis) and Class C (e.g. valium, steroids). Some of these drugs can be <u>prescribed</u> by doctors as <u>medicines</u>.

2) The <u>penalties</u> for <u>possessing</u> and <u>supplying</u> Class A drugs are much harsher than those for Class B and Class C drugs. E.g., the police don't usually arrest people for possession of Class C drugs unless they suspect an '<u>intent to supply</u>'. Supplying Class A drugs carries a maximum penalty of <u>life imprisonment</u>.

3) These classifications are because some drugs are more <u>dangerous</u> than others. In general, Class A drugs are highly <u>addictive</u>, cause serious psychological or physical <u>damage</u> and are easy to <u>overdose</u> on (see 'Problems' below).

Age-Restricted Drugs: Alcohol and Tobacco

1) It's illegal to <u>sell tobacco or alcohol</u> to people under the age of 18.

2) That <u>doesn't</u> mean it's illegal for you to drink or smoke under 18 — you're just not allowed to buy them yourself. In theory, that means the decision to let you drink or smoke is made by <u>responsible adults</u>.

3) Campaigners argue that alcohol and tobacco are as <u>addictive</u> and <u>harmful</u> as many illegal drugs, so it's <u>inconsistent</u> for some to be legal and others not. Some people use this as an argument for the <u>criminalisation</u> of tobacco or <u>tighter</u> controls on alcohol. Others use it to argue that other 'social' drugs that are currently illegal (e.g. cannabis) should be <u>legalised</u>.

Drugs can Cause Health and Social Problems

Most drugs are <u>addictive</u> — either <u>physically</u> or <u>psychologically</u>, or <u>both</u>. An addiction is a <u>compulsion</u> to keep doing something, even if you know it's harming you. A <u>physical addiction</u> is where your body chemistry has been changed by the drug, so you get <u>withdrawal symptoms</u> if you stop taking it. A <u>psychological addiction</u> is where you <u>crave</u> the feeling the drug gives you, and get anxious or depressed without it.

SOCIAL PROBLEMS

1) Most drugs affect people's <u>judgement</u>, which can make them more likely to take <u>risks</u>.

2) People on a 'high' sometimes feel <u>invincible</u>, and dangerous activities like <u>sharing needles</u> and <u>unprotected sex</u> are more likely to happen under the influence of drink or drugs.

3) Some addicts <u>stop caring</u> about other aspects of their life, and ignore their <u>responsibilities</u>.

4) At the <u>extreme</u>, some addicts turn to <u>crime</u> to help fund their habit.

HEALTH PROBLEMS

1) Different drugs cause different health problems.

2) <u>Alcohol</u>, if drunk in excess, can cause <u>liver disease</u>, <u>brain damage</u>, and <u>heart failure</u>. It also doesn't <u>mix</u> well with other drugs. Even a small dose of some drugs mixed with alcohol can <u>kill</u>.

3) Smoking <u>cannabis</u> can cause <u>lung diseases</u> in a similar way to smoking tobacco. Recent studies have also suggested that it might trigger <u>psychological disorders</u> in vulnerable people.

4) <u>Hallucinogens</u> like LSD and 'magic mushrooms' can cause permanent <u>psychological damage</u>.

5) The biggest health risks with <u>heroin</u> are <u>overdose</u>, <u>diseases transferred by needle sharing</u> (e.g. HIV) and <u>poisoning</u> by other things it's cut (mixed) with. The drug itself doesn't cause much damage in small doses, but <u>deaths</u> from overdose are <u>very common</u>.

Are you feeling lucky — well are you... punk...

One of the biggest dangers in buying drugs off the street is that you never actually know what's in them. A bag of white powder sold as cocaine could be mixed with anything from local anaesthetic to rat poison.

Drugs and Alcohol: Religious Views

I suppose we'd better have the religious take on all this now — this is Religious Studies, after all.

Christianity, Judaism and Islam all say Drugs are Bad

1) *"Your body is a temple of the Holy Spirit..."* — although this is a line from the New Testament (1 Corinthians 6:19), the message is similar for Christianity, Islam and Judaism. Drugs are seen as bad, as they damage the mind, abuse the body God has given to us, and can lead to poverty or even death.

2) Hard drugs (e.g. heroin and cocaine) and hallucinogens are completely disapproved of by Christianity, Judaism and Islam. They're seen as a way of escaping the realities of life, and existing instead in an artificial fantasy world.

3) They're also illegal, and all religions teach that you should obey the laws of the land you're living in (see page 23).

4) All three religions teach that the mind and the body are gifts from God, and that we do not have the right to abuse them. On a more practical level, drug taking is also seen as leading to irresponsible behaviour (e.g. neglecting your family or responsibilities), and possibly criminal activity.

5) Drugs taken to enhance performance in sport are also disapproved of, as they do not allow a person to properly display the skills they have been given. Again, they create a false world.

6) Islam is against cannabis for the same reasons it's against alcohol (see below). And Sheikh Ibn Taymiyyah (a famous scholar and Islamic teacher) had this to say on the subject: *"Sinful people smoke hashish (i.e. cannabis)... it disturbs the mind and temperament... excites sexual desire."*

The Religions have Different Views on Alcohol

1) Most Christian denominations allow the consumption of alcohol — it's used in Holy Communion after all. However, drunkenness is frowned on, and some denominations are more disapproving than others.

   MODERATIONISTS (e.g. Roman Catholics, Anglicans and Lutherans) argue that alcohol is a gift from God to be enjoyed in moderation (while being aware of its dangers). Jesus and the Apostles drank wine at the last supper, and wine has always been used in Holy Communion.

   ABSTENTIONISTS (e.g. Methodists and the Salvation Army) believe that alcohol can be a bad influence, and so it's not wise to drink it. In Proverbs 31:4-7, the Bible says that alcohol can make you forget your responsibilities. Abstentionists don't believe alcohol is inherently evil though.

   PROHIBITIONISTS (e.g. Seventh Day Adventists) believe that drinking alcohol is a sin. They argue that all references in the Bible to Jesus and the Apostles drinking wine referred to grape juice.

2) In Judaism, alcohol is permitted, although drinking to excess is disapproved of. The Midrash (a collection of moral stories) contains the line, *"wine enters, sense goes out."*

3) Alcohol is forbidden in Islam, as it causes people to lose control — it's seen as a weapon of Shaytan (the Devil). People are more likely to do stupid things when they're drunk, and stop thinking about other people or Allah. A Muslim should have a clear mind when praying, and so there can be no place for alcohol.

4) Tobacco isn't mentioned in the Torah or the Qur'an — not surprising, as it hadn't been discovered when they were written. However, it's harmful to the body, and so should really be avoided.

So I take it Jimi Hendrix wasn't a Muslim then...

This is a big social issue, so you'd expect every religion to have something to say on the matter. But as with all Religion and Society topics, come exam time, you'll need to give your own opinions too. That's what makes this subject interesting — sometimes there are no right or wrong answers, just different opinions.

Practice Questions

So don't break the law — it's naughty and you'll get busted. Don't sin — you'll go to hell. Don't take drugs — unless you've got a death wish (jury's out on the alcohol front, though). And here endeth the lesson.

But before you go, there's that minor issue of the exam. If you can answer all these questions without breaking a sweat, you'll be well set come exam day. If you get stuck on any of these, look back at the section and then try again. Don't give up until you can answer them all.

1) What is:
   a) a crime?
   b) a sin?
   c) a law?
   d) justice?
   e) deterrence?
   f) reform?
   g) rehabilitation?
   h) capital punishment?
   i) addiction?

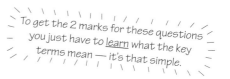
To get the 2 marks for these questions you just have to learn what the key terms mean — it's that simple.

2) For each of the following questions, give two reasons for your point of view.
   a) Do you think it's important to follow law?
   b) Do you think punishment can act as a deterrent?
   c) Do you agree with capital punishment?
   d) Do you think drugs should be illegal?
   e) Do you think drinking alcohol is always bad?

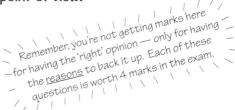
Remember, you're not getting marks here for having the 'right' opinion — only for having the reasons to back it up. Each of these questions is worth 4 marks in the exam.

3) For these questions, take extra care with your spelling, punctuation and grammar, and express yourself as clearly as possible.
   a) Explain why justice is important to Christians.
   b) Choose one religion other than Christianity and explain why justice is important to its followers.
   c) Explain why some Christians support the use of capital punishment and others do not.
   d) Choose one religion other than Christianity and explain its teachings on drugs.
   e) Explain why some Christians allow the drinking of alcohol and others do not.

If you're struggling with the structure of your answer, have a look at page 30. These are worth 8 marks each in the exam, so they're important.

4) Read the following statements:
   a) "Religious people should always obey the law."
   b) "For religious people, the aim of punishment should be rehabilitation."
   c) "Religious people should oppose capital punishment."
   d) "Religious people shouldn't drink alcohol."

   For each statement:
   (i) Do you agree? Give reasons for your opinion.
   (ii) Give reasons why some people may disagree with you.
   In your answers you should refer to at least one religion.

This lot of questions should remind you that you need to learn both sides of the big arguments — no matter how passionately you believe in your own opinion. 3 marks for your opinion — 3 marks for someone else's.

Do Well in Your Exam

You've learnt all the <u>facts</u> — now it's time to get those <u>grades</u>.

You'll have a 1½ Hour Exam on Religion and Society

1) For the Religion and Society exam you'll have to answer a question on <u>each</u> of the <u>four topics</u> — <u>Rights and Responsibilities</u>, <u>Environmental and Medical Issues</u>, <u>Peace and Conflict</u>, and <u>Crime and Punishment</u>.

2) For each topic you'll have the choice of <u>two questions</u>. Each question is worth <u>20 marks</u> and will be split into <u>four parts</u>. You have to answer <u>all four parts</u> of each question you choose.

3) For part (<u>c</u>) of each question you'll be marked in part on your <u>use of English</u> — this means you need to use top quality <u>spelling</u>, <u>punctuation</u> and <u>grammar</u> — and proper <u>formal</u> language. Don't forget to use all the <u>fancy words</u> you've learned during the course.

There are Easy Marks for Knowing What Things Mean

Two marks out of each question are for just knowing what the <u>important words mean</u>. These questions don't carry a lot of marks, so keep your answers <u>short</u> and <u>to the point</u> — but make sure you define the word <u>properly</u>. You need to learn all the terms from the glossary.

> a)   What is **pacifism**?   (2 marks)

The idea that violence and war are wrong under any circumstances. ← **Try to answer this kind of question in one sentence.**

This is too long. You <u>don't have time</u> to write an essay on questions that don't offer many marks. Keep your answer short and to the point. → Pacifism is a belief that physical violence and war are totally wrong under any circumstances. Pacifists believe that all disputes should be settled peacefully. Christian pacifists argue that violence goes against Jesus's teachings to love one's enemy and 'turn the other cheek'.

But this is just an example, not a definition, so it'd only get you 1 mark. → Conscientious objectors are pacifists.

You'll be asked about What you Think

There's <u>no right answer</u> to this kind of question — only <u>good answers</u> that'll get you <u>lots of marks</u> and <u>bad answers</u> that <u>won't</u>. The difference between the two is that good answers give <u>clearly developed reasons</u>. You can make reference to the <u>religious teachings</u> you have studied, but in part (<u>b</u>) you <u>don't have to</u>.

> b)   Do you think governments should be able to limit freedom of speech?
>   Give two reasons for your point of view.
>   (4 marks)

Freedom of speech is one of the fundamental human rights laid down by the United Nations. If we lose one of those rights, others might follow.
Freedom of speech allows people to debate important issues, and to argue against decisions they do not agree with.

Both of these answers are pretty good despite arguing different things from different perspectives.

Make sure you back up each point with a relevant reason.

Try to use proper sentences. You won't get extra marks for it on this question — but it'll make it easier for the person marking your paper. → Freedom of speech gives people the right to say anything they like about other people, even if it is hurtful, so it isn't always a good thing.
Governments should be able to take away the freedom of speech of people who would encourage violence, to protect the rest of society.

Nobody told me anything about thinking...

Don't forget — you don't get marks for what you believe, only for the reasons you give to back up your opinions. So make sure you know all the main arguments, for all the big topics.

Do Well in Your Exam

More stuff for you on the <u>exam</u> right here. Get <u>stuck in</u>.

<u>You'll have to</u> <u>Explain Why...</u>

1) For the part (<u>c</u>) question, you'll get some marks for the <u>quality</u> of your <u>written English</u>. This includes your <u>spelling</u>, <u>punctuation</u> and <u>grammar</u>.

2) You'll also get marks for using the kind of <u>fancy words</u> that you'll find in the <u>glossary</u> — learn what they <u>mean</u>, how to <u>use</u> them, and how to <u>spell</u> them.

Best break out the best handwriting for this one.

> c) Choose one religion, and explain why some of its followers are in favour of infertility treatment in some circumstances, but not in others. **(8 marks)**

You'd only use Judaism as an example if you'd studied it during the course.

Jewish teachings place importance on having a family. It says in Genesis that God commanded "<u>Be fruitful and increase in number; fill the earth...</u>". However, the use of infertility treatment would only be approved of for <u>heterosexual</u>, <u>married</u> couples, as this is seen as the proper context for raising children.

In-vitro fertilisation and <u>artificial insemination</u> are allowed as long as both the egg and the sperm come from the married couple, but using donated sperm is usually frowned upon, as it can be seen as a form of <u>adultery</u>. Egg donation is allowed, though many Jewish people prefer the egg to come from a <u>Jewish</u> woman. This is because, according to Orthodox teachings, you are only a Jew if your <u>mother</u> is a Jew.

It won't hurt i **you remember** **little bit of** **scripture.**

3) If you <u>structure</u> your answer well you'll get more marks — so <u>sketch</u> out a <u>plan</u> before you write out your answer.

4) The best marks will go to those who put in a <u>number</u> of reasons and/or <u>develop</u> their reasons well.

5) To get top marks, you usually have to give either '*four brief reasons, three reasons with one developed, two developed reasons or a comprehensive explanation using one reason only*'. So if you've only got one point to make in an answer like this, you'd better make sure you know it inside out.

> c) Explain why the followers of one religion believe that war is justified sometimes, but not always. **(8 marks)**

You'll get marks for using 'specialist vocabulary' — i.e. Jihad

Muslims believe that a <u>lesser Jihad</u>, such as war, is <u>justified</u> if it will bring about freedom from tyranny, stop oppression, or right injustices. It is <u>not justified</u> if its aim is to colonise a country, or force non-believers to become Muslim. Its goal must always be <u>peace</u>.

War is only justified if it is declared by a <u>religious leader</u> and it must always be fought in the name of Allah. One Hadith says "<u>He who fights that Allah's Word should be superior fights in Allah's cause</u>". If someone dies in a war fought for Allah, they will become a martyr and be rewarded by going straight to Paradise.

You'd only use Islam as an example if you'd studied it during the course.

It can be good to put your best point last.

<u>Thou shalt write clearly...</u>

As much as you may know every little fact that pops up in this book, a large chunk of how well you do in exams will come down to, well..., how good you are at exams. Make sure you spend enough time reading through these pages, and enough time practising doing exam-style questions under timed conditions. It'll all pay off in the end.

Do Well in Your Exam

Here's a page on those pesky questions where you have to understand <u>other people's opinions</u>.

You need to know *Both Sides* of the *Argument*

1) In part (<u>d</u>) you'll get the <u>same marks</u> for writing what <u>you think</u> and for writing what people who <u>disagree</u> with you think. So spend the <u>same time</u> and <u>effort</u> on each.

2) You'll be told to refer to a <u>religion</u> here, so make sure you do. If you don't do this in at least one part of your answer, you can only score a maximum of half marks.

> d) "Alcohol is related to thousands of deaths each year. It should be made illegal."
> In your answer you should refer to at least one religion.
> (i) Do you agree? Give reasons for your opinion. (3 marks)
> (ii) Give reasons why some people may disagree with you. (3 marks)

(i) I <u>do not</u> believe that alcohol should be made illegal. Many people drink alcohol in moderation, and it causes no harm. It would be wrong to stop them enjoying themselves. The law already restricts the sale of alcohol to over 18s, so this protects children who cannot make informed choices.

<u>Moderationists</u> believe that alcohol is a gift from God. Jesus and the apostles drank wine at the <u>Last Supper</u>, and Jesus said we should drink it in remembrance of him — that is why it is used in <u>Holy Communion</u>.

If it was made illegal, people would still use it, but in secret, which may make <u>social problems</u> worse.

(ii) Some people would argue that alcohol is just as harmful and addictive as many illegal drugs, so it is inconsistent for it to not be illegal. It can cause liver disease, brain damage and heart failure.

<u>Christians</u>, <u>Jews</u> and <u>Muslims</u> would all claim that our minds and bodies are gifts from God, and we have no right to abuse them. In the New Testament it says "<u>your body is a temple of the Holy Spirit</u>".

Alcohol can make people act irresponsibly, and they may do stupid things, such as have unprotected sex. Muslim people believe that alcohol is a weapon of <u>Shaytan, the Devil</u>.

> **Try to make the reasons why people disagree with you as good as the reasons for your own opinion.**

(i) I believe that alcohol <u>should</u> be made illegal. It is as harmful and addictive as cannabis which is a Class B drug, so it should be made illegal too. As well as causing serious illnesses, drink-driving kills people. This would be much less likely if alcohol was not freely available. If there were harsh punishments for drinking alcohol, most people would not take the risk of drinking it. Even though it is illegal for people under 18 to buy alcohol, many young people get hold of alcohol and drink too much of it.

(ii) Some people would argue that many people are responsible drinkers and enjoy drinking alcohol in sensible amounts. They would claim that they find alcohol helps them to relax, and that it would be unfair to punish them because some people abuse alcohol. Alcohol has been legal for a long time, so it would cause a lot of anger if it was suddenly made illegal. Also, if people want to drink, it is their choice — it is their bodies that they are damaging.

> **This answer will lose marks because it doesn't refer to a specific religion in either part.**

> **Don't waffle. If you keep your answer more to the point, you'll get more in. And that means more marks.**

> **If you can only think of one reason in the exam, make sure you develop it as best you can.**

Don't forget the *Basics*

1) Read the questions <u>carefully</u>. Make sure you <u>read both questions</u> on each topic before you pick one of them. Remember, you've got to answer <u>all the parts</u> of the questions you pick.

2) Be aware of how much <u>time</u> you're using. If you've got a bit left at the end <u>read through</u> your answers.

"I think exams are rubbish" — "I think exams are great..."

...but that's just because they pay me to put revision guides together. Make sure you learn the different arguments for both sides of the key issues. It's not a bad lesson to take away from the exam — even if you believe something strongly, it's worthwhile knowing why other people don't. You might even change your mind...

Glossary

addiction	**A compulsion to keep doing something, even if you know it's harming you.** _Addiction can be physical (i.e. you'll suffer physical discomfort, 'withdrawal symptoms', if you stop) or psychological (i.e. you crave the thing you're addicted to)._
aggression	**In war, this means attacking someone without provocation.** _Acts of aggression violate international law._
artificial insemination	**Injecting sperm (either the husband's or a donor's) directly into a woman's womb.** _Artificial insemination by the husband (AIH) is often the first step in treating infertility._
Bible	**The holy text of the Christian religion, made up of the Old Testament (the Jewish Bible) and the New Testament** _(the Gospels and letters written by early Church leaders)._
bullying	**Intimidating, frightening and controlling people who are weaker than you.**
capital punishment	**The death penalty as punishment for a crime.**
Church	**The community of all Christians — also often used to refer to a particular community, e.g. the Roman Catholic Church.** _A place of worship is a church with a lower case 'c'._
conflict resolution	**Bringing a war to an end in a way that leads to a lasting peace.**
conscience	**An inner feeling of what's right and what's wrong. Some Christians believe that your conscience is the 'voice of God'.**
conservation	**Protecting and preserving resources, particularly natural resources and the environment in general.**
creation	**The act of making something, or the thing that has been made. In Religious Studies, this usually refers to the creation of the Universe by God/Allah/The Almighty.**
crime	**An act that breaks a state law.**
the Decalogue	**The Ten Commandments, as listed in Exodus 20.** _These commandments are the basic rules for leading a moral life._
democratic processes	**Any ways in which citizens can take part in the running of a country, e.g. voting, protesting, joining pressure groups or political parties.**
deterrence	**The idea that if a punishment is sufficiently bad in some way, it will put people off (or deter them from) committing the crime.** _This is the idea behind telling people in advance what the punishment for a given crime is — so they understand the consequences._
electoral processes	**Ways in which voting is organised.** _In the UK, every citizen over 18 has the right to vote. Voting is by secret ballot, and most elections use the 'first past the post' electoral system._
embryo	**A fertilised egg in the first eight weeks after fertilisation. (After eight weeks, the embryo becomes a foetus.)**
environment	**The surroundings in which we (and all other animals and plants) live, and that we depend on for survival.**
exploitation	**Taking advantage of a weaker person or group of people.**

Glossary

forgiveness	Stopping being angry with someone about something they've done wrong.
global warming	The increase in the temperature of the Earth over the past century. It's thought to be caused by the release of greenhouse gases into the atmosphere.
the Golden Rule	The verse from Matthew's Gospel that says, 'So in everything, do to others what you would have them do to you'. Christians believe that this sums up Jesus's teachings on moral responsibility.
human rights	The moral, legal and political rights that every human being on Earth is entitled to. They give basic freedoms (e.g. freedom from violence, freedom from slavery) and protection to people around the world.
infertility	Not being able to have children.
in-vitro fertilisation	An infertility treatment in which eggs and sperm are mixed in a test tube until fertilisation takes place, then a resulting embryo is transplanted into the woman's womb to develop.
judgement	Coming to a conclusion about the merits of something. In the context of both law courts and judgement by God, this means deciding the guilt or innocence of someone and determining their appropriate punishment or reward.
justice	The idea of each person getting what they deserve, and maintaining what's right. In the context of law, that means making sure the guilty are suitably punished and the innocent are protected.
just war	A war that's fought in a just cause, as a last resort, with a good chance of success, and with proportionality (any harm it causes is less than the harm it's trying to prevent). And that's fought in a way that minimises civilian casualties.
law	A rule made by Parliament and enforced by the courts that's designed to protect people's rights.
natural resources	Anything found naturally in the environment that's useful to humans, e.g. metals, oil for fuel and plastics, fertile land for growing crops.
organ donation	Giving organs to be transplanted into someone else. Some organs (e.g. kidneys) can be donated from a living donor. Most organs are donated after death. People who wish to be organ donors after death put their names on the Organ Donor Register.
pacifism	The idea that war and physical violence are wrong under any circumstances. Pacifists believe that all disputes should be settled peacefully.
political party	A group of (usually) like-minded people who try to get elected to government based on their policies, e.g. Labour, the Conservatives and the Liberal Democrats.
pressure group	An organisation that tries to influence government decisions on particular issues, e.g. Greenpeace or the Stop the War Coalition.
reconciliation	When people, or groups of people, that used to be opposed to each other come together to make peace. It's more than just not fighting any more, though — it's about ending up on friendly terms.

Glossary

reform	The idea that punishment should aim to change criminals so that they won't reoffend once their punishment is over.
rehabilitation	**Preparing someone for a return to a normal life.** In terms of punishment, this is the idea that an offender should be given education, training and counselling to help them lead a useful life once their punishment is over.
respect	Showing consideration for other people and their feelings.
responsibility	Having to answer for your own actions. A responsibility is also a duty to do something or care for someone.
retribution	The idea that punishment is a way of taking revenge on someone, of making them 'pay' for an injury they've caused.
sin	An act that breaks a religious law, i.e. when God's teaching is disobeyed.
Situation Ethics	A Christian ethical principal based on the idea that the only intrinsically good thing is Christian love. When making a decision, we should choose to do the most loving thing.
social change	The way in which the structure, behaviour and attitudes of society have changed and are changing (and the potential for change in the future).
stewardship	Taking care of something, e.g. of the Earth as custodians of creation, so that it can be passed on to the next generation.
surrogacy	**When a woman bears a child for another woman.** A surrogate is often used to help a woman who can't carry a child to term for whatever reason (e.g. she has no womb).
the United Nations	An international organisation set up after World War II to promote peaceful solutions to disputes, to encourage global cooperation and to protect people's human rights.
weapons of mass destruction	Weapons that can destroy large areas of land and/or lots of people all at once, e.g. chemical, biological and nuclear weapons.
world peace	An end to all violent conflict, all over the world.

Index

Index